THE MOST
POWERFUL
PRAYERS
OF ALL TIME

THE MOST POWERFUL PRAYERS OF ALL TIME

MAIA DAGUERRE

WordCrafts

The Most Powerful Prayers of All Time
Copyright © 2016
Maia Daguerre

Cover concept & design by David Warren

All rights reserved. No part of this book may be reproduced, stored in a retrieval system, or transmitted in any form or by any means – electronic, mechanical, photocopy, recording, or otherwise – without the prior written permission of the publisher. The only exception is brief quotations for review purposes

Published by WordCrafts Press
Buffalo, Wyoming 82834
www.wordcrafts.net

Contents

Dedication i
Thanks ii
Foreword iii
Preface v
Introduction vii
Previous Considerations viii

Chapter I
  THE SPIRIT SPEAKS 1

The Vision of Enoch 2
Always we hope 5
Mind precedes all mental states 6
The Ten Commandments 7
Native American Ten Commandments 8
Offer only lovely things on my altars 9
I tell you, keep asking, and it will be given you 10
Valedictory Address 11
But I tell you who hear: 12
The Tract of The Quiet Way 13
For everything there is a season, ... 17
The brightness of the sun, ... 18
Shema Israel 19
"I" Am The "I" 21
Tao never acts, yet nothing is left undone. 22
Full of equanimity 23
God in All Things 24
The Golden Verses of Pythagoras 25
Listen! Do not let your time pass idly. 30
Remain faithful to the earth, my brothers, ... 31

Chapter II
  REVERENCE 32

Surya Namaskar Mantra 33
Take Lord, ... 34
Salat 35
In a Thousand Forms 36

Five-Pointed Daily Prayer of Worship..................................37
O Krishna, it is right 39
I pray to Thee, Almighty God,..40
Surah Al-Fatiha 41
Hymn To Amun-Ra 42
I bow to the One who has no color,..43
Psalm 8: 1-9...44
O Lord Jesus Christ,..45
To The Creative God..46
God, there is no God but He,..47
Late have I loved you,..48
Address to Supreme Deity...49
The Lord's Prayer...50

Chapter III
   GUIDANCE..**51**

Lord, make me an instrument of Thy peace...........................52
God's Aid...53
Khatum..54
O Great Spirit,..55
Serenity Prayer...56
Salat al-Istikharah 57
Grandfather, ...58
The Wesley Covenant Prayer 59
God of our life,..60
O Lord!..61
Heavenly Father,..62
Make Us Worthy 63
Universal Prayer 64
Prayer to Our Lady of Guadalupe...65
Lord, teach me to pray...66
I cannot dance, O Lord,...67
Lead me from the unreal 68
I am of the nature to grow old. 69

Chapter IV
   FORGIVENESS...**70**

Forgive me, O Lord; 71
Lesson 122 72

Forgiveness offers everything I want. 72
Father, Forgive them; 73
To recite after Salat Alan-Nabi: 74
Prayer for Repentance 75
Forgive me, most gracious Lord and Father, ... 76
Praise be unto Thee, O Lord. 77
Forgiving Father, forgive us for our sins. 78
O Lord, remember not only the men 79
The Litany of Reconciliation 80
O God, forgive the poverty, ... 81
Our Lord, do not mind us 82
Ho'oponopono Mantra 83

Chapter V
    AWAKENING 84

Bodhisattva Prayer for Humanity 85
May I be at peace. 86
Looking behind, I am filled with gratitude. 87
Nirvanashatkam 88
Song of Vibhuti Yoga 90
Contemplation on No-Coming and No-Going 91
Oracle of Sumiyoshi (Prayer of Benevolence) 92
I see no stranger, I see no enemy. 93
Be generous in prosperity, ... 94
First I Thank the Source of All Life 95
Golden Chain 96
And I think over again. 97
O cosmic power! 98
Birth is a beginning and death a destination: 99
Prayer when opening a door 100
Prayer on building a wall 101
O lord my God, ... 102
O Jesus, my feet are dirty. 103
That is perfect. 104
A Warrior's Creed 105

Chapter VI
    MOTHER EARTH 107

Hymn to The All-Mother 108

Four Directions Prayer 109
Sláva 111
Though my heart desires shield flowers, ... 112
O our Father, the Sky, ... 113
The Canticle of the Creatures 114
May all I say 115
O Lord, O God, Creator of our land, ... 116
Dadirri is deep listening 117
Grandfather, Great Spirit, ... 118
The mountains, I become a part of it... 119
Invocation to The U'wannami 120
The Prayer for the Earth 121
Water flows over these hands. 122
The garden is rich with diversity, ... 123
Through the Silence of Nature 124
O our Mother the Earth, ... 125
Four Elements Medicine Wheel 126
HaShem: 128
Hymn XXX - To Earth the mother of all 129
But ask the animals, now, and they shall teach you; 130

Chapter VII
   ABUNDANCE **131**

Prayer for Sustenance 132
Hoshbam (Prayer at Dawn) 133
O God, when I have food, ... 134
Pir 135
Ode 279 136
He is the One who sent down water from the sky 137
Psalm 35:27 138
Prayer of The Sower 139
It's Harvest Time 140
Every time I feel the spirit 141
The Radical Empowerment PowerShift Process 142
Lord Jesus Christ, you are the sun 144
Prayer to Lord Ganesh 145
Blessed are we 146

Chapter VIII
  GRATITUDE 147

We give thanks for all those who are moved, ... 148
The sun brings forth the beginning. 150
Invocation to Ormazd 151
Thanksgiving Day Prayer 152
Lord we Praise You for cities and towns, ... 153
Ohen:ton Karihwatehkwen. 154
("The Words that Come Before All Else") 154
The Blessing of Unanswered Prayers 158
Great and Eternal Mystery of Life, ... 159
If the only prayer you said. 160
Let us be grateful to people who make us happy; 161
We return thanks to our mother, the earth, ... 162
O My Father, Great Elder, ... 163

Chapter IX
  HEALING 164

First Epistle to the Corinthians - Chapter 13 165
Nayaz 166
Prayer to the World 167
O Allah! I am your servant, ... 168
Invocation 169
Heavenly Father, ... 170
Exorcism of Spirits of Disease 171
When the wind blows. 172
Violet Flame Decrees - Healing 173
The Guest House 176
And I saw the river 177
I cleanse myself of all selfishness, ... 178
The great sea moves me, sets me adrift. 179
Hymn to The Unknown God 180
God stir the soil. 182
Our Hands Imbibe Like Roots 183
O Supreme and unapproachable Light! 184

Chapter X
PEACE 185

Let us know peace. 186
As wind carries our prayers 187
The fruit of silence is prayer... 188
Lord of Peace, Divine Ruler, ... 189
Deep within the still center of my being, ... 190
I am peace, ... 191
Litany for Peace 192
O! Thou God of all beings, ... 193
Deep peace I breathe into you, ... 194
Pray not for Arab or Jew, ... 195
Christ, why do you allow wars 196
The Peace Of "I" 197
Peace Invocations 198
Silence 199

Chapter XI
PROTECTION 200

Hymn to Cihuacoatl 201
Traditional Consecration Prayer
   to St Michael the Archangel 202
Saint Patrick's Breastplate 203
Walk in Beauty 206
Prayer of Light 207
The Great Invocation 208
Psalm 23 209
I, the servant of God, will make fast thrice 210
Dua Qu'nut 211
Psalm 27:1-13 212
Tube of Light 214
Magical Incantation 215
Each day and each night 216
I, God, am in your midst. 217
That Wondrous Star 218

Chapter XII
SALVATION 220

Hail Holy Queen.. 221
Stenatlihan, You are good!................................... 222
One in spirit,.. 223
Litany of the Most Precious Blood of Our Lord Jesus Christ 224
Dowa 226
Anima Christi 227
I have no other helper than you, no other father. 228
Clash... 229
Lord Jesus Christ, whose will all things obey: 230
Save me, God, from the distraction 231
Aren't you going too far, Lord............................... 232
The Seven-Limb Prayer 233
Our God, our help in ages past,........................... 234
I know the path: it is strait and narrow. 236

Chapter XIII
BLESSINGS 237

Offering the Mandala... 238
The Blessing of Light, Rain and Earth 239
Peace Pilgrim's Beatitudes 240
May every creature abound 241
The Sermon on the Mount................................... 242
May penetrating light dispel the darkness 243
Blessed is the spot, ... 244
Bless my enemies, O Lord................................... 245
A Birthday Prayer.. 247
The Four Immeasurables..................................... 248
Dedication of Merit 249
Priestly Blessing 251

Chapter XIV
BLESSING THE DAY 252

O Mother Earth,... 253
I am awake,... 254
Morning Consecration to Mother Mary 255
Listen to the exhortation of the dawn! 256

As watchmen wait for the morning, ... 257
Chapter XV
   BLESSING THE NIGHT AND THE DREAMS 258

Oh Lord 259
In Thy name, Lord, I lay me down 260
I reverently speak 261
Blessed are you, Lord our God, ... 262
Be our light in the darkness, O Lord, ... 263
Father of Heaven, whose goodness has brought 264
O Allah! 266
Watch thou, dear Lord, ... 267
Chapter XVI
   HOUSE BLESSINGS 268

Into whatever house you enter, ... 269
O heavenly Father, Almighty God, ... 270
God bless the corners of this house, ... 271
Birkat HaBayit 272
Great Spirit, ... 273
O my guardians, from remote antiquity, ... 274
Chapter XVII
   MEAL BLESSINGS 275

Bless all of those who have brought this 276
Blessed are You, Lord our God, ... 277
Now that I am about to eat, ... 278
This ritual is one 279
The food which we are about to eat 280
Round the table 281
Innumerable labors brought us this food; 282
Chapter XVIII
   SAFE JOURNEY 283

You, O God, are the Lord of the mountains 284
Tefilat HaDerech 285
May the road rise to meet you 286
When biding farewell 287

Chapter XIX
  FACING DEATH **288**

Preserving the Heart 289
O Creator of men 290
Do not stand at my grave and forever weep 291
El Malei Rachamim 292
Bind the sick man to Heaven, ... 293
Blessing 294
Confession on a Death-Bed 295
Prayer of Transformation into a Lotus 296
O Saint Joseph whose protection is so great, ... 297

Chapter XX
  INVOCATIONS OF THE POETS **298**

The Fruit of the Tree 299
It is pure jade, a wide plumage, your heart, ... 300
In the place of tears, I, the singer, ... 301
Keep off your thoughts from things 302
Measure for Measure 303
Hamlet 303
Part One: Life / LIII 304
A Suspended Blue Ocean 305
Impermanence 306
A Meditation in Time of War 307
Prayer 308
God Full of Mercy 310
Where are the tidings of union? that I may arise- 311
What is this atom which contains the whole, ... 312
Spring 313
Buddha in Glory 314
The Worm's Waking 315
Image of God 316
I am not I 317
Let me not pray to be sheltered from dangers 318
O Thou transcendent, ... 319
The Divine Image 321
No coward soul is mine, ... 322
The moon shines in my body, ... 323

Under One Small Star 324
God 326
Notes and Acknowledgments 327
About the Author 334
Index of Titles and First Lines 335
Index of Authors, Sources and Themes 343

Dedication

This book is dedicated to my family, who taught me the taste for praying; to my spiritual guides, who, from unknown dimensions, light my way and pray for me; and to all those who, by praying throughout the ages, sought their way back home.

Thanks

Clarice Violet, my first safe haven in the United States.

Ena and Howard, and their sacred space-time, where this book was whispered.

Joshua and Carol, blessed bridges.

Doug Collins, DM Collins and Danielle Hampson for opening paths.

Walter Daguerre, true love.

Foreword

What is prayer but a calling to the creative intelligence which abides within us? This creative intelligence is known by many different names and speaks to our deepest most inner self - our souls. With the distractions created by our busy lives many have lost the connection with the greatest part of ourselves, our inner sanctuary where all our real power lies. We put so much importance in our outer world losing sight of what is most precious, our relationship with our creator of all creations.

Prayer brings us back to our source. It comforts us in times of tribulation. It reminds us that there is something far greater than who we are. Through the prayers that Maia Daguerre has put together we are reminded of this beautiful gift we have been given which is the profound relationship we can develop with the creative intelligence who is with us all the time.

This book will help us practice the presence of this almighty force. Prayer can open our hearts so we can hear that small voice within us. It will guide us to a more joyful and loving life. It will give us a greater understanding of the holiness of this creative force and how it touches our lives if we would only recognize it. These prayers will help us heal our suffering and the suffering of others and teach us about the most powerful gift that we can give to ourselves and others.

We will learn that through mercy and kindness bestowed upon us we can give these gifts to one another. In this world where there is so much fear, anger and hatred let these words spoken here teach us about love, compassion and forgiveness. Let us learn how to rise about the differences that divide us and bathe in the energies that unite us. Let us learn to walk in the wondrous beauty that surrounds us every day and which these prayers remind of us of, and let us respect this great mystery which has breathed life in everyone of us. May we learn through these prayers to have love for all beings, and let these prayers bring a message of hope to everyone.

This is a book to behold, to be cherished and to use often to remind us of our connection with the all powerful. It is a book which will remind us of God's presence and it is a book which can give us great comfort, peace, solace and will uplift your soul. The words of these prayers can not only help in the time of need, these prayers will touch the heart and soul of all those who read them.

Maia Daguerre has touched upon all aspects of what is important to our own personal inner growth. Taken from all spiritual traditions these prayers serve as an inspiration and a vehicle to transcend our human ego and to experience the sublime. In a world where the greatest problem is a disconnection with one another Maia Daguerre reminds us that the way back home, the way to re-connect and to know our interconnection with one another, is through the act of prayer.

The prayers shared within these pages become a road map to our own spiritual essence, the truth of who we are. These words will open our hearts to the true joy and happiness life has to offer and will help us realize that what is most important is our relationship with our creative source. We are blessed with the gift that Maia Daguerre brings to us in this collection of prayers. If you allow these prayers into your heart, you will feel the comfort, guidance, courage and wisdom of these words. There is no greater gift than that.

And so my prayer for all of you who have been blessed to be reading this book is that the messages here reaches far and wide, illuminating the spirit that resides within all of us, reminding us that the whole of humanity truly is interconnected with one another guided by a an unseen force whose greatness shines the most beautiful light upon all of us.

Dr. Eileen R. Borris
Licensed Psychologist
Author of **Finding Forgiveness** *(McGraw-Hill, 2010)*
President, Forgiveness International
Director of Training, The Institute for Multi-Track Diplomacy

Preface

You recognize a seeker through her eyes. And so, at first glance, I recognized her. From her mouth, sophisticated concepts are translated with simplicity and poetry. Even for the toughest existential questions, Maia Daguerre always finds support in some thinker, scientist, philosopher, poet, turning an arid subject in a pleasant and exciting conversation. Were not enough, there is the music. Singer and songwriter, she uses her verses to compose scenarios that go beyond words, making the notes, the rhythm and the melody take command of a greater meaning.

A seeker is, before all, a curious. Maia Daguerre is the kind of person who strives to go deep into her research. With her sharp mind, she follows the clues found in her readings, and with her trusting heart, she gets carried away by intuition and feelings. With this, Maia Daguerre can always go one step further than most people, crossing data collected from the most remote civilizations to the most daring scientific theories.

The questions that Maia makes herself are her way of being in the world and her legacy, after all. She prefers to move by doubt, by accurate observation, through questioning. And her first target is her own being: Who is this "I" that thinks itself, feels and desires? Such questions reverberate in her physical body, her emotional field and, inevitably, in her spirit. That's where comes her fascination with the immaterial.

But Maia's spirituality has nothing to do with religion. Her soul is too free to let it be tied by dogmas. Her interest is comprehensive, generous and so embraces all expressions that connect to God.

Prayers - she says - are passwords to access the divine. So no matter whether they were uttered by a Jewish Messiah in ancient Galilee, for a Persian Sufi poet in the century XIII, or a rock star on stage somewhere in the 60's in California... If they are manifestations of inherent human desire to awake and to ascend, she will consider them.

Interestingly, despite the commitment, she does not get lost trying to find the perfect, ideal response. Her work is first and foremost an affirmation of life, with all its deficiencies, detours and mishaps. And it is this non-linear trajectory that causes us to fall in Love with her quest, we identify with it. In the end, we fell in love with her passion.

"The Most Powerful Prayers of All Time" is a fascinating book. Let these prayers that Maia compiled with so much love, care and dedication serve as a set of windows to let the light and fresh air of God renew your vows of faith in life.

Walter Daguerre
Playwright, Screenwriter and Film Director

Introduction

A book with the most powerful prayers of all time is never finished. Either because there is always the possibility of some prayer having been left out, or because the very act of praying will never end - constantly toasting us with more material, new and renovated. Everything is always evolving.

Just as prayer is part of humanity since the beginning of time, praying is part of my life since the beginning of my existence. Since the Catholic novenas which I participated in my childhood, through the meditation groups of different traditions that I joined in my youth, to my yoga and Kabalah practices, - and later, when I seriously fought with God and began to deny Him - until my involvement in neo shamanic groups recently, the ecumenical practice has always been part of my life. And always will. Talk - and listen - to God has always been one of my greatest blessings, even when I did not believe in His existence. Today I know that in the depths of my heart.

This is a book that I always searched for on the shelves. And as I didn't find it, I wrote it. Now, it became a gift for you, the reader of this fascinating and mysterious twenty-first century.

May this book serve as a bridge for the expansion of your consciousness. May it lead us towards the end of the barriers that prevent us from seeing ourselves as a great brotherhood of beings, sharing the same pulsating planet. May it deepen your spiritual journey in this amazing adventure that is human life.

Maia Daguerre

Previous Considerations

As mentioned in the introduction, this research work is inexhaustible, especially when it aims to bring together ancient texts and information not readily available for research. Any prayer that has not been included in this collection can always be added in future editions - I would be grateful to receive more material - and any mistake will be corrected in due course.

Some prayers here are very well known and, per se, quite powerful. For obvious reasons, I could not include all the famous ones. Others prayers were considered powerful from my point of view. In this sense, my selection is personal, and therefore arbitrary. There's a Brazilian proverb that says: "Always leave to the heart the final word." And so I did.

As far as possible, I tried to encompass prayers of all formally known traditions. And I ask the reader to be opened for the beautiful messages of this book, and give less attention to its form, but to the content of it.

The criterion for the inclusion of certain prayers in certain chapters was based in the understanding of the overall message they bring, not in the words of their text or title. Thus, some prayers construed as "for peace", for example, in my opinion and for the purpose of this collection, worked better as a healing, or an awakening prayer.

The chapter "Invocations of the Poets" is my tribute to Poetry. Poems are always prayers, and in this case, for a loved one called God, though apparently is not only the love for Him what poets are singing here. Whenever we turn ourselves to God, we always do it for one single reason. Ultimately, all songs, all acts, all words and all human thoughts can be summarized to a single feeling: a call for love.

Maia Daguerre

"O gods! All your names and forms are to be revered, saluted, and adored; all of you who have sprung from heaven, and earth, listen here to my invocation."

Rig- Veda X, 63, 2

"Prayer never goes in vain. So long as no response is received, prayer must be continued."

Anandamayi Ma

"Grant us grace, almighty Father, so to pray as to deserve to be heard."

Jane Austen

Chapter I

THE SPIRIT SPEAKS

Maia Daguerre

The Vision of Enoch

I speak to you.
Be still
Know I am God.

I spoke to you when you were born.
Be still
Know I am God.

I spoke to you at your first sight.
Be still
Know I am God.

I spoke to you at your first word.
Be still
Know I am God.

I spoke to you at your first thought.
Be still
Know I am God.

I spoke to you at your first love.
Be still
Know I am God.

I spoke to you at your first song.
Be still
Know I am God.

I speak to you through the grass of the meadows.
Be still
Know I am God.

I speak to you through the trees of the forests.
Be still
Know I am God.

I speak to you through the valleys and the hills.
Be still
Know I am God.

I speak to you through the Holy Mountains.
    Be still
    Know I am God.

I speak to you through the rain and snow.
    Be still
    Know I am God.

I speak to you through the waves of the sea.
    Be still
    Know I am God.

I speak to you through the dew of the morning.
    Be still
    Know I am God.

I speak to you through the peace of the evening.
    Be still
    Know I am God.

I speak to you through the splendor of the sun.
    Be still
    Know I am God.

I speak to you through the brilliant stars.
    Be still
    Know I am God.

I speak to you through the storm and the clouds.
    Be still
    Know I am God.

I speak to you through the thunder and lightening.
    Be still
    Know I am God.

I speak to you through the mysterious rainbow.
    Be still
    Know I am God.

I will speak to you when you are alone
    Be still
    Know I am God.

Maia Daguerre

> I will speak to you through the Wisdom of the Ancients.
> Be still
> Know I am God.
>
> I will speak to you at the end of time.
> Be still
> Know I am God.
>
> I will speak to you when you have seen my Angels.
> Be still
> Know I am God.
>
> I will speak to you throughout Eternity.
> Be still
> Know I am God.
>
> I speak to you.
> Be still
> Know I am God.

Essene Gospel from the Dead Sea Scrolls

Always we hope
someone else has the answer.

Some other place will be better,
some other time it will all turn out.

This is it.

No one else has the answer.
No other place will be better,
and it has already turned out.

At the center of your being you have the answer;
you know who you are
and you know what you want.

There is no need
to run outside for better seeing.

Nor to peer from a window.

Rather abide at the center of your being;
for the more you leave it
the less you learn.

Search your heart
and see
the way to do
is to be.

Attributed to Lao Tzu (6th century BCE)

Maia Daguerre

Mind precedes all mental states.

Mind is their chief;
they are all mind-wrought.

If with an impure mind
a person speaks or acts
suffering follows him
like the wheel that follows
the foot of the ox.

Mind precedes all mental states.

Mind is their chief;
they are all mind-wrought.

If with a pure mind
a person speaks or acts
happiness follows him
like his never-departing shadow.

Excerpt from "The Dhammapada"
Collection of sayings of the Buddha in verse form and one of the most widely read and best known Buddhist Scriptures

The Ten Commandments

God spoke all these words, saying, "I am Yahweh your God, who brought you out of the land of Egypt, out of the house of bondage.

"You shall have no other gods before me.

"You shall not make for yourselves an idol, nor any image of anything that is in the heavens above, or that is in the earth beneath, or that is in the water under the earth: you shall not bow yourself down to them, nor serve them, for I, Yahweh your God, am a jealous God, visiting the iniquity of the fathers on the children, on the third and on the fourth generation of those who hate me, and showing loving kindness to thousands of those who love me and keep my commandments.

"You shall not take the name of Yahweh your God in vain, for Yahweh will not hold him guiltless who takes his name in vain.

"Remember the Sabbath day, to keep it holy. You shall labor six days, and do all your work, but the seventh day is a Sabbath to Yahweh your God. You shall not do any work in it, you, nor your son, nor your daughter, your male servant, nor your female servant, nor your livestock, nor your stranger who is within your gates; for in six days Yahweh made heaven and earth, the sea, and all that is in them, and rested the seventh day; therefore Yahweh blessed the Sabbath day, and made it holy.

"Honor your father and your mother, that your days may be long in the land which Yahweh your God gives you.

"You shall not murder.

"You shall not commit adultery.

"You shall not steal.

"You shall not give false testimony against your neighbor.

"You shall not covet your neighbor's house. You shall not covet your neighbor's wife, nor his male servant, nor his female servant, nor his ox, nor his donkey, nor anything that is your neighbor's."

From the Book of Exodus 20: 1-17 (6th / 4th century BCE)

Maia Daguerre

Native American Ten Commandments

1. Treat the Earth and all that dwell thereon with respect.
2. Remain close to the Great Spirit.
3. Show great respect for your fellow beings.
4. Work together for the benefit of all Mankind.
5. Give assistance and kindness wherever needed.
6. Do what you know to be right.
7. Look after the well being of mind and body.
8. Dedicate a share of your efforts to the greater good.
9. Be truthful and honest at all times.
10. Take full responsibility for your actions.

Unknown Author

Offer only lovely things on my altars
– The bread of life, and jewels, and feathers and flowers.

Let the streams of life flow in peace.

Turn from violence.

Learn to think for a long time
how to change this world
and how to make it better to live in.

All the people in the world
ought to talk about it
and speak well of it always.

Then it will last forever,
and the flowers will bloom forever
and I will come to you again.

Aztec Prayer (14th / 16th century CE)

Maia Daguerre

I tell you, keep asking, and it will be given you.

Keep seeking, and you will find.

Keep knocking, and it will be opened to you.

For everyone who asks receives.

He who seeks finds.

To him who knocks it will be opened.

Which of you fathers, if your son asks for bread, will give him a stone?

Or if he asks for a fish, he won't give him a snake instead of a fish, will he? Or if he asks for an egg, he won't give him a scorpion, will he?

If you then, being evil, know how to give good gifts to your children, how much more will your heavenly Father give the Holy Spirit to those who ask him?

From the Gospel of Luke 11:9-13 (1st century CE)

Valedictory Address

Speak what is true.

Do your duties.

Continue, without neglect, the daily study of the Veda.

Do not swerve from Truth and Dharma, and do something useful in the social economy.

Achieve greatness, and do not fail to refresh your memory in respect of what you have learnt.

Remember the Gods and your ancestors.

Look upon your mother as God.

Look upon your father as God.

Honor your teacher as God.

Honor your guest as if God came to receive your attention.

May you ever exercise your understanding, and, distinguishing the good from the blame-worthy, avoid the latter, and ever do what is good.

Follow all that was good in your teacher's life, not any other.

You will meet with better men and women than even the teachers with whom you have lived.

Show them due respect.

Traditional Hindu Text

Maia Daguerre

But I tell you who hear:

love your enemies, do good to those who hate you, bless those who curse you, and pray for those who mistreat you. To him who strikes you on the cheek, offer also the other; and from him who takes away your cloak, don't withhold your coat also. Give to everyone who asks you, and don't ask him who takes away your goods to give them back again.

As you would like people to do to you, do exactly so to them. If you love those who love you, what credit is that to you? For even sinners love those who love them. If you do good to those who do good to you, what credit is that to you? For even sinners do the same. If you lend to those from whom you hope to receive, what credit is that to you? Even sinners lend to sinners, to receive back as much. But love your enemies, and do good, and lend, expecting nothing back; and your reward will be great, and you will be children of the Most High; for he is kind toward the unthankful and evil.

Therefore be merciful,
    even as your Father is also merciful.

Don't judge,
    and you won't be judged.

Don't condemn,
    and you won't be condemned.

Set free,
    and you will be set free.

Give, and it will be given to you: good measure, pressed down, shaken together, and running over, will be given to you. For with the same measure you measure it will be measured back to you.

From the Gospel of Luke 6:27-38 (1ˢᵗ century CE)

The Tract of The Quiet Way

The Lord says:

For seventeen generations I have been incarnated as a high mandarin, and I have never oppressed my people nor maltreated my subordinates. I have helped them in misfortune; I have rescued them from poverty; I have taken compassion on their orphans; I have forgiven their transgressions; I have extensively practiced secret virtue, which is attuned to heaven above. If you are able to keep your hearts as I have kept mine, Heaven will surely bestow upon you blessings. Therefore, these are the instructions I declare unto mankind:

He who wants to expand the field of happiness, let him lay the foundation of it on the bottom of his heart.

Practice benevolence wherever you find an opportunity, and let your deeds of merit be unheeded

Benefit all creatures; benefit the people.

Practice goodness: acquire merit.

Be honest like Heaven in conducting your affairs.

Compassionate and auspicious, the state government must be devoted to the salvation of the people.

Let your heart be impartial and wide of range.

Fulfil the four obligations; impartially observe the three doctrines.

Be faithful and reverential to the ruler. Be filial and obedient to parents. Be congenial and friendly to brothers. Be sincere in your intercourse with friends.

Let some worship the Truthful One, and revere the Northern Constellation, while others bow before the Buddha and recite sutras.

By discoursing on morality and righteousness, convert both the cunning and the dull. By preaching on the canonical books and histories, enlighten the ignorant and the benighted.

Relieve people in distress as speedily as you must release a fish from a dry rill (lest he die). Deliver people from danger as quickly as you must free a sparrow from a tight noose.

Be compassionate to orphans and relieve widows. Respect the old and help the poor.

Promote the good and recommend the wise. Be lenient with others and exacting with yourself.

Save your clothing and provisions that ye may befriend the hungry and cold on the road.

Give away coffins and cases lest the dead of the poor be exposed.

Build charitable graveyards for unclaimed corpses.

Establish philanthropic institutions for the education of children.

If your own family is well provided, extend a helping hand to your relatives. If the harvest fails, provide for and relieve your neighbors and friends.

Let measures and scales be accurate; and be neither chary in selling nor exacting in buying.

Treat your servants with generosity and consideration. Do not expect perfection nor be too strict in your demands.

Publish and make known sutras and tracts. Build and repair temples and shrines.

Distribute medicine to alleviate the suffering of the sick. With tea or water relieve the distress of the thirsty.

Light lanterns in the night to illuminate where people walk. Keep boats on rivers to ferry people across.

Buy captive animals and give them freedom.

How commendable is abstinence that dispenses with the butcher!

While walking be mindful of worms and ants.

Be cautious with fire and do not set mountain woods or forests ablaze.

Do not go into the mountain to catch birds in nets, nor to the water to poison fishes and minnows.

Do not butcher the ox that plows thy field.

Do not throw away paper that is written on.

Do not scheme for others' property.

Do not envy others' accomplishments.

Do not approach thy neighbor's wife or maids.

Do not stir thy neighbors to litigation.

Do not injure thy neighbor's reputation or interest.

Do not meddle with thy neighbor's conjugal affairs.

Set not, for personal malice, brothers at variance with one another.

Set not father and son at variance for trifles.

Never take advantage of your power, nor disgrace the good and law-abiding.

Presume not, ye that are rich; nor deceive the needy and suffering.

While attending to your duty, be humble and modest.

Live in concord with your relatives and clansmen.

Let go hatred and forgive malice.

Those that are good seek ye for friends; that will help you to practice virtue with body and soul. Those that are wicked keep at a distance; it will prevent evil from approaching you.

Pass in silence over things wicked, but promulgate all that is good.

Do not assert with your mouth what your heart denies.

Always have in mind helpful sayings.

Do not use improper language.

Cut the brambles and thorns that obstruct the highway. Remove bricks and stones that lie in the path.

Repair the defiles though for many hundred years they have remained unimproved.

Build bridges to be traversed by thousands and ten thousands of people.

Expound moral maxims to correct the people's faults.

Supply the means to give instruction to people of talent.

Let your work conform to Heaven's reason, and let your speech express humaneness.

Keep the ancient sages before your eyes even when at supper or while looking over the fence.

Be mindful when you are alone in the shadow of your coverlet.

Anything evil refrain ye from doing; all good deeds do! So will you be released forever from the influence of evil stars, and always be encompassed by good guardian angels.

Rewards may be immediate, and you will receive them in person, or rewards may be remote, and will devolve upon your posterity.

Blessings come a hundredfold in loads as if drawn by horses; good fortune is piled up a thousand-fold like a mass of clouds.

Do not all these things accrue to the heart of the quiet way?

Classic Taoist Text
From the book "Yin Chih Wen"(1600)
Translated by Teitaro Suzuki and Paul Carus (1906)

The Yin Chih Wen is a religio-ethical tract read, studied and taught both in schools and at the home in China. Its contents are very little known in the Western world.

For everything there is a season,
and a time for every purpose under heaven:

a time to be born,
    and a time to die;
a time to plant,
    and a time to pluck up that which is planted;

a time to kill,
    and a time to heal;
a time to break down,
    and a time to build up;

a time to weep,
    and a time to laugh;
a time to mourn,
    and a time to dance;

a time to cast away stones,
    and a time to gather stones together;
a time to embrace,
    and a time to refrain from embracing;

a time to seek,
    and a time to lose;
a time to keep,
    and a time to cast away;

a time to tear,
    and a time to sew;
a time to keep silence,
    and a time to speak;

a time to love,
    and a time to hate;
a time for war,
    and a time for peace.

From the Book of Ecclesiastes 3:1-8 (3rd century BCE)

Maia Daguerre

The brightness of the sun,
which lights up the world, the brightness of the moon and of fire - these are my glory.

With a drop of my energy I enter the earth and support all creatures.

Through the moon, the vessel of life-giving fluid, I nourish all plants.

I enter breathing creatures and dwell within as the life-giving breath.

I am fire in the stomach which digests all food.

Entering into every heart, I give the power to remember and understand;

It is I again who take that power away.

All the scriptures lead to me; I am their author and their wisdom.

The Bhagavad Gita, 15:12-15
Traditionally ascribed to the Sage Ved Vyasa, the Bhagavad Gita is a 700-verse scripture, part of the Hindu epic Mahabharata. In this chapter, called "The Yoga of the Supreme Person," Lord Krishna explains the full scope of the presence of the Absolute.

Shema Israel

(Cover your eyes with your right hand and say): Hear, O Israel, the L-rd is our G-d, the L-rd is One.

(Recite the following verse in an undertone): Blessed be the name of the glory of His kingdom forever and ever.

You shall love the L-rd your G-d with all your heart, with all your soul, and with all your might.

And these words which I command you today shall be upon your heart.

You shall teach them thoroughly to your children, and you shall speak of them when you sit in your house and when you walk on the road, when you lie down and when you rise.

You shall bind them as a sign upon your hand, and they shall be for a reminder between your eyes.

And you shall write them upon the doorposts of your house and upon your gates.

And it will be, if you will diligently obey My commandments which I enjoin upon you this day, to love the L-rd your G-d and to serve Him with all your heart and with all your soul, I will give rain for your land at the proper time, the early rain and the late rain, and you will gather in your grain, your wine and your oil.

And I will give grass in your fields for your cattle, and you will eat and be sated.

Take care lest your heart be lured away, and you turn astray and worship alien gods and bow down to them.

For then the L-rd's wrath will flare up against you, and He will close the heavens so that there will be no rain and the earth will not yield its produce, and you will swiftly perish from the good land which the L-rd gives you.

Therefore, place these words of Mine upon your heart and upon your soul, and bind them for a sign on your hand, and they shall be for a reminder between your eyes.

You shall teach them to your children, to speak of them when you sit in your house and when you walk on the road, when you lie down and when you rise.

And you shall inscribe them on the doorposts of your house and on your gates - so that your days and the days of your children may be prolonged on the land which the L-rd swore to your fathers to give to them for as long as the heavens are above the earth.

(The L-rd spoke to Moses, saying): Speak to the children of Israel and tell them to make for themselves fringes on the corners of their garments throughout their generations, and to attach a thread of blue on the fringe of each corner.

They shall be to you as *tzitzit*, and you shall look upon them and remember all the commandments of the L-rd and fulfill them, and you will not follow after your heart and after your eyes by which you go astray - so that you may remember and fulfill all My commandments and be holy to your G-d.

I am the L-rd your G-d who brought you out of the land of Egypt to be your G-d; I, the L-rd, am your G-d.

Traditional Jewish Prayer
Centerpiece of the morning and evening Jewish prayer services, "Hear, O Israel" are the first two words of a section of the Torah, the sacred book of the Jews and their most important declaration of faith and a pledge of allegiance to God.

"Tzitzit" are the fringe tassels attached to the four corners of the tallit (prayer shawl) and tallit katan (everyday undergarment). Their strings and knots are a physical representation of the Torah's do's and don'ts.

"I" Am The "I"

"I" come forth from the void into light,
"I" am the breath that nurtures life,
"I" am that emptiness, that hollowness beyond all consciousness,
The "I", the *Id*, the All.

"I" draw my bow of rainbows across the waters,
The continuum of minds with matters.

"I" am the incoming and outgoing of breath,
The invisible, untouchable breeze,
The undefinable atom of creation.

"I" am the "I".

Morrnah Nalamaku Simeona (1913–1992)
Hawaiian healer

Simeona taught her updated version of Hoʻoponopono, an ancient Hawaiian practice of reconciliation and forgiveness, throughout the United States, Asia and Europe. Modern practitioners of Hoʻoponopono use the mantra "I love you. I'm sorry. Please forgive me. Thank you." as a way of getting to the state of no memories and no identity.

"I" is the Roman numeral I, representing the oneness of the Universe.

Maia Daguerre

Tao never acts, yet nothing is left undone.

~

The great Tao flows everywhere;
It can go left; it can go right.
The myriad things owe their existence to it,
And it does not reject them.
When its work is accomplished,
It does not take possession.
It clothes and feeds all,
But does not pose as their master.
Ever without ambition,
It may be called Small.
All things return to it as their home,
And yet it does not pose as their master,
Therefore it may be called Great.
Because it would never claim greatness,
Therefore its greatness is fully realized.

Attributed to Lao Tzu (6th century BCE)
Excerpts from "Tao Te Ching", the Chinese classic text of Taoism

Full of equanimity
Of benevolent thought
Of tender thought
Of affectionate thought
Of useful thought
Of serene thought
Of firm thought
Of unbiased thought
Of undisturbed thought
Of unagitated thought
Of thought fixed on the practice of discipline
                                  and transcendent wisdom
Having entered on knowledge
                        which is a firm support to all thoughts
Equal to the ocean in wisdom
Equal to the mount *Meru* in knowledge
Rich in many good qualities
They attain perfect wisdom.

Buddhist Prayer
From the "Sukhavativyuha Sutra"

"Mount Meru" is a sacred mountain with five peaks in Hindu, Jain and Buddhist cosmology and is considered to be the center of all the physical, metaphysical and spiritual universes.

Maia Daguerre

God in All Things

Apprehend God in all things, for God is in all things.
Every single creature is full of God and is a book about God.
Every creature is a word of God.
If I spent enough time with the tiniest creature – even a caterpillar –
I would never have to prepare a sermon,
so full of God is every creature.

Meister Eckhart (1260–1328)
German Theologian, Philosopher and Mystic

The Golden Verses of Pythagoras

1. First worship the Immortal Gods, as they are established and ordained by the Law.

2. Reverence the Oath, and next the Heroes, full of goodness and light.

3. Honor likewise the Terrestrial Dæmons by rendering them the worship lawfully due to them.

4. Honor likewise thy parents, and those most nearly related to thee.

5. Of all the rest of mankind, make him thy friend who distinguishes himself by his virtue.

6. Always give ear to his mild exhortations, and take example from his virtuous and useful actions.

7. Avoid as much as possible hating thy friend for a slight fault.

8. Understand that power is a near neighbor to necessity.

9. Know that all these things are as I have told thee; and accustom thyself to overcome and vanquish these passions:

10. First gluttony, sloth, sensuality, and anger.

11. Do nothing evil, neither in the presence of others, nor privately;

12. But above all things respect thyself.

13. In the next place, observe justice in thy actions and in thy words.

14. And accustom not thyself to behave thyself in any thing without rule, and without reason.

15. But always make this reflection, that it is ordained by destiny that all men shall die.

16. And that the goods of fortune are uncertain; and that as they may be acquired, so may they likewise be lost.

17. Concerning all the calamities that men suffer by divine fortune,

18. Support with patience thy lot, be it what it may, and never repine at it.

19. But endeavor what thou canst to remedy it.

20. And consider that fate does not send the greatest portion of these misfortunes to good men.

21. There are among men many sorts of reasonings, good and bad;

22. Admire them not too easily, nor reject them.

23. But if falsehoods be advanced, hear them with mildness, and arm thyself with patience.

24. Observe well, on every occasion, what I am going to tell thee:

25. Let no man either by his words, or by his deeds, ever seduce thee.

26. Nor entice thee to say or to do what is not profitable for thyself.

27. Consult and deliberate before thou act, that thou mayest not commit foolish actions.

28. For it is the part of a miserable man to speak and to act without reflection.

29. But do that which will not afflict thee afterwards, nor oblige thee to repentance.

30. Never do anything which thou dost not understand.

31. But learn all thou ought'st to know, and by that means thou wilt lead a very pleasant life.

32. In no wise neglect the health of thy body;

33. But give it drink and meat in due measure, and also the exercise of which it has need.

34. Now by measure I mean what will not incommode thee.

35. Accustom thyself to a way of living that is neat and decent without luxury.

36. Avoid all things that will occasion envy.

37. And be not prodigal out of season, like one who knows not what is decent and honorable.

38. Neither be covetous nor niggardly; a due measure is excellent in these things.

39. Do only the things that cannot hurt thee, and deliberate before thou dost them.

40. Never suffer sleep to close thy eyelids, after thy going to bed,

41. Till thou hast examined by thy reason all thy actions of the day.

42. Wherein have I done amiss? What have I done? What have I omitted that I ought to have done?

43. If in this examination thou find that thou hast done amiss, reprimand thyself severely for it;

44. And if thou hast done any good, rejoice.

45. Practice thoroughly all these things; meditate on them well; thou oughtest to love them with all thy heart.

46. 'Tis they that will put thee in the way of divine virtue.

47. I swear it by him who has transmitted into our souls the Sacred Quaternion, the source of nature, whose cause is eternal.

48. But never begin to set thy hand to any work, till thou hast first prayed the gods to accomplish what thou art going to begin.

49. When thou hast made this habit familiar to thee,

50. Thou wilt know the constitution of the Immortal Gods and of men.

51. Even how far the different beings extend, and what contains and binds them together.

52. Thou shalt likewise know that according to Law, the nature of this universe is in all things alike,

53. So that thou shalt not hope what thou ought'st not to hope; and nothing in this world shall be hid from thee.

54. Thou wilt likewise know, that men draw upon themselves their own misfortunes voluntarily, and of their own free choice.

55. Unhappy that they are! They neither see nor understand that their good is near them.

56. Few know how to deliver themselves out of their misfortunes.

57. Such is the fate that blinds mankind, and takes away his senses.

58. Like huge cylinders they roll to and fro, and always oppressed with ills innumerable.

59. For fatal strife, innate, pursues them everywhere, tossing them up and down; nor do they perceive it.

60. Instead of provoking and stirring it up, they ought, by yielding, to avoid it.

61. Oh! Jupiter, our Father! If Thou would'st deliver men from all the evils that oppress them,

62. Show them of what dæmon they make use.

63. But take courage; the race of man is divine.

64. Sacred nature reveals to them the most hidden mysteries.

65. If she impart to thee her secrets, thou wilt easily perform all the things which I have ordained thee.

66. And by the healing of thy soul, thou wilt deliver it from all evils, from all afflictions.

67. But abstain thou from the meats, which we have forbidden in the purifications and in the deliverance of the soul;

68. Make a just distinction of them, and examine all things well.

69. Leaving thyself always to be guided and directed by the understanding that comes from above, and that ought to hold the reins.

70. And when, after having divested thyself of thy mortal body, thou arrivest at the most pure Æther,

71. Thou shalt be a God, immortal, incorruptible, and Death shall have no more dominion over thee.

Pythagoras (6th century BCE)
Greek philosopher and Mathematician

From "The Golden Verses of Pythagoras And Other Pythagorean Fragments: Selected and Arranged by Florence M. Firth" (1904)

Maia Daguerre

Listen! Do not let your time pass idly.

Either keep a rosary with you and do japa;
Or if this does not suit you, at least go on repeating the Name of the Lord regularly, and without interruption, like the ticking of a clock.
There are no rules or restrictions in this.
Invoke Him by the Name that appeals to you most, for as much time as you can – the longer the better.
Even if you get tired or lose interest, administer the Name to yourself like a medicine that has to be taken.
In this way, you will, at some auspicious moment, discover the rosary of the mind, and then you will continually hear within yourself the praises of the great Master, the Lord of Creation, like the never ceasing music of the boundless ocean;
You will hear the land and the sea; the air and the heavens reverberate with the song of His glory.
This is called the all-pervading Presence of His Name.

Anandamayi Ma (1896–1982)
Indian Saint from Bengal

From "Ma's Teaching in Her Own Words" at www.srianandamayima.org

The Spirit Speaks

Remain faithful to the earth, my brothers,
with the power of your virtue. Let your gift-giving love and your knowledge serve the meaning of the earth. Thus I beg and beseech you. Do not let them fly away from earthly things and beat with their wings against eternal walls. Alas, there has always been so much virtue that has flown away. Lead back to the earth the virtue that flew away, as I do—back to the body, back to life, that it may give the earth a meaning, a human meaning.

Friedrich Nietzsche (1844-1900)
German Philosopher

From the book "Thus Spoke Zarathustra" (1883)

Chapter II

REVERENCE

Surya Namaskar Mantra

Salutations to Him who is my friend.
Salutations to Him who is the cause for change.
Salutations to Him who propels everyone into activity.
Salutations to Him who is in the form of light.
Salutations to Him who moves in the Sky.
Salutations to Him who nourishes all.
Salutations to Him who contains everything.
Salutations to Him who possesses rays.
Salutations to Him who is the son of Aditi.
Salutations to Him who produces everything.
Salutations to Him who is fit to be worshipped.
Salutations to Him who is the cause of luster.

Traditional Hindu Prayer

"Surya Namaskar" (the Sun Salutation) is chanted audibly or mentally while performing a series of 12 specific poses (asanas) of the Yoga Tradition. It is done in the early morning facing the rising sun or in the evening facing the setting sun.

Maia Daguerre

Take Lord,
and receive all my liberty,
my memory, my understanding,
and my entire will, all that I have and possess.

Thou hast given all to me.
To Thee, O lord, I return it.

All is Thine,
dispose of it wholly according to Thy will.

Give me Thy love and thy grace,
for this is sufficient for me.

Saint Ignatius Loyola (1491–1556)
Theologian founder of the "Society of Jesus" (Jesuits)

Excerpt from the book "The Spiritual Exercises"

Salat

Most gracious Lord, Master, Messiah, and Savior of Humanity, we greet Thee with all humility.

Thou art the First Cause and the Last Effect, the Divine Light and the Spirit of Guidance, Alpha and Omega.

Thy Light is in all forms, Thy Love in all beings: in a loving mother, in a kind father, in an innocent child, in a helpful friend, in an inspiring teacher.

Allow us to recognize Thee in all Thy holy names and forms; as Rama, as Krishna, as Shiva, as Buddha.

Let us know Thee as Abraham, as Solomon, as Zarathushtra, as Moses, as Jesus, as Mohammed, and in many other names and forms, known and unknown to the world.

We adore Thy past; Thy presence deeply enlighteneth our being, and we look for Thy blessing in the future.

O Messenger, Christ, Nabi, the Rasul of God!

Thou whose heart constantly reacheth upward, Thou comest on earth with a message, as a dove from above when Dharma decayeth, and speakest the Word that is put into Thy mouth, as the light filleth the crescent moon.

Let the star of the Divine Light shining in Thy heart be reflected in the hearts of Thy devotees.

May the Message of God reach far and wide, illuminating and making the whole humanity as one single Family in the Parenthood of God.

Amen.

Inayat Khan (1882 – 1927)
Indian Musician, Mystic Philosopher and Founder of the Sufi Movement

Maia Daguerre

In a Thousand Forms

You may hide yourself in a thousand forms,
Still, All-beloved, I recognize you;
You may cover yourself in magic mists,
All-present, I can always tell that it is you.

I discover you as well, All-beautifully-growing,
In the cypress's pure young surge,
In the stream's fresh, living rush,
All-enchanting, I know you well.

When rising jets of water unfurl,
All-playful, how glad I am to see you;
When clouds form and transform themselves,
All-manifold, I discern you in them.

In the blossoming tapestry that covers the meadow,
I see your All-colorful, starry beauty;
When ivies reach their thousand arms around,
I meet you, All-embracing.

When morning lights the mountain range
I greet you there too, All-brightening,
Then, as the sky grows round above me,
All-heart-expanding, it is you I inhale.

What, with out and inner senses, I know,
I know only through you, All-teaching;
When I name Allah's hundred names,
A name, with each name, re-echoes for you.

Johann Wolfgang von Goethe (1749 –1832)
German writer

Translated by John White (1809–1893)

Five-Pointed Daily Prayer of Worship

Early morning

O Giver of Light,
the Cosmic Beauty,
permeate my whole nature
with Thy Rays.
Kindle the flame
on the altar of my temple
so that I may live
as a beam of light,
in beauty,
until the sunset of the day
of my life.

9:00 a.m.

O Sphere of Light,
advancing and elevating
Goodness,
may my soul
rise with You,
expressing goodness
in all its contacts.

Noon

The flame of the Great Presence in me,
Let me stand
as a radiant fire
of righteousness
today
and during the days
of my life.
Let me think, act and speak
in the spirit of righteousness.

Maia Daguerre

Sunset

My Lord,
thank You for the joy
of living today
in the spirit of beauty,
goodness,
and righteousness.
May Your joy
radiate in other parts of the world,
as the Sun
disperses the night
and brings the joy of the day.
My Lord,
You are the joy of my heart.

Bedtime

My Lord, let Your freedom
permeate my whole being.
let me be free
from all worries and anxieties,
from all painful memories
of the day,
from all attachments and identifications,
so that my soul freely soars,
in Your temple of beauty.
Let me realize freedom
from my physical,
emotional
and mental crystallizations,
And be with You as a free soul.

Torkom Saraydarian (1917–1997)
Armenian author

From the book "A Daily Discipline of Worship"

Reverence

O Krishna, it is right

that the world delights and rejoices in your praise, that all the saints and sages bow down to you, and all evil flees before you, to the far corners of the universe.

How could they not worship you, O Lord?

You are the eternal spirit, who existed before Brahma, the creator, and who will never cease to be, the Lord of the gods, you are the abode of the universe.

Changeless, you are what is and what is not, and beyond the duality of existence and nonexistence.

You are the first among gods, the timeless spirit, the resting place of all beings.

You are the knower and the thing which is known.

You are the final home; within your infinite form you pervade the cosmos.

You are Vayu, god of wind; Yama, god of death; Agni, god of fire; Varuna, god of water.

You are the moon and the creator Prajapati, and the great-grandfather of all creatures.

I bow before you and salute you again and again.

You are behind me and in front of me; I bow to you on every side.

Your power is immeasurable.

You pervade everything; you are everything.

Excerpt from "The Bhagavad Gita", 11:36-40 (5th / 2nd century BCE)

Traditionally ascribed to the sage Ved Vyasa, the Bhagavad Gita is a 700-verse scripture, part of the Hindu epic Mahabharata. In this chapter, Arjuna talks, in state of astonishment and ecstasy, after seeing the universal form of Lord Krishna.

Maia Daguerre

I pray to Thee, Almighty God,
Jah Rastafari,
King of Kings, Lord of Lords,
Conquering Lion of the Tribe of Judah.

That the words of mine own mouth,
as well as the meditations of mine own heart,
be acceptable in thy sight.

That thou givest me strength in my hour of weakness,
wisdom in my hour of foolishness,
patience in my hour of vex,
understanding in my hour of confusion,
grace and forgiveness in my hour of judgment.

Selah...

Traditional Rastafari Prayer

Selah is used in Iyaric Rastafarian vocabulary and can be heard at the end of some reggae songs. Its usage is to accentuate the magnitude and importance of what has been said, and often is a sort of substitute for "Amen."

Surah Al-Fatiha

In the name of Allah, The Most Gracious, The Most Merciful:
All Praise is due to Allah, Lord of the Universe,
The Most Gracious, The Most Merciful,
Owner of the Day of Judgment.

You alone we worship,
And You alone we turn to for help.

Guide us to the straight path,
The path of those on whom You have bestowed your grace,
Not of those who have earned Your anger,
Nor of those who went astray.

Traditional Islamic Prayer (7th century CE)

Sura Al-Fatiha (The Opening) is the first chapter of the Quran and it has a special role in the Muslim daily prayers ("Salat"), being recited at the start of each unit of prayer, or "rak'ah."

Maia Daguerre

Hymn To Amun-Ra

Hail to Thee, Amun-Ra, lord of the thrones of the earth, the oldest existence, ancient of heaven, support of all things;

Chief of the gods, lord of truth, father of the gods, maker of men and beasts and herbs, maker of all things above and below;

Deliverer of the sufferer and oppressed, judging the poor, lord of wisdom, lord of mercy, most loving, opener of every eye, source of joy, in whose goodness the gods rejoice, thou whose name is hidden.

Thou art the one, maker of all that is, the one, the only one, maker of gods and men; giving food to all.

Hail to Thee, Thou one with many heads, sleepless when all others sleep, adoration to Thee.

Hail to Thee from all creatures from every land, from the height of heaven, from the depth of the sea.

The spirits Thou hast made extol Thee, saying:

Welcome to Thee, father of the fathers of the gods, we worship Thy spirit which is in us.

Ancient Egyptian Prayer

From "Pagan Prayers" by Marah Ellis Ryan (1913)

I bow to the One who has no color,

I bow to the One who has no beginning.

I bow to the One who is without fault,

I bow to the One who is incomprehensible.

I bow to the One who has no treasure,

I bow to the One who is indestructible.

I bow to the Bountiful.

I bow to the Unlimited.

Sacred Song Of The Sikhs

Sikhism is a monotheistic religion founded during the 15th century in the Punjab region of South Asia

Maia Daguerre

Psalm 8: 1-9

Yahweh, our Lord, how majestic is your name in all the earth,
> who has set your glory above the heavens!

From the lips of babes and infants you have established strength,
> because of your adversaries, that you might silence the enemy and the avenger.

When I consider your heavens, the work of your fingers,
> the moon and the stars, which you have ordained;

What is man, that you think of him?
> What is the son of man, that you care for him?

For you have made him a little lower than God,
> and crowned him with glory and honor.

You make him ruler over the works of your hands.
> You have put all things under his feet:

All sheep and cattle,
> yes, and the animals of the field,
> the birds of the sky, the fish of the sea,
> and whatever passes through the paths of the seas.

Yahweh, our Lord,
> how majestic is your name in all the earth!

Attributed to King David (10th century BCE)
From "The Book of Psalms"

O Lord Jesus Christ,

I long to live in your presence,
to see your human form
and to watch you walking on earth.

I do not want to see you
through the darkened glass of tradition,
nor through the eyes of today's values and prejudices.

I want to see you as you were,
as you are,
and as you always will be.

I want to see you as an offense to human pride,
as a man of humility,
walking amongst the lowliest of humanity,
and yet as the savior and redeemer
of the human race.

Søren Kierkegaard (1813–1855)

Danish philosopher, theologian, poet and social critic, widely considered to be the first existentialist philosopher

Maia Daguerre

To The Creative God

O Lord of Charms, Illustrious! Who gives
Life to the dead, the Merciful who lives
And grants to hostile gods of Heaven return,
To homage render, worship thee, and learn

Obedience!
Thou who didst create mankind
In tenderness, Thy love round us, O wind!
The Merciful, the God with whom is Life
Establish us, O Lord, in darkest strife
O never may Thy truth forgotten be.
May Accad's race forever worship thee!

Akkadian Invocation (17th century BCE)
Semitic empire of ancient Mesopotamia

God, there is no God but He,
the Living, the Sustainer.

No slumber or sleep overtakes Him;
to Him belongs all that is in heavens
and in the Earth.

Who will intercede with Him except by His leave?

He knows their present and their future,
and they do not have any of His knowledge
except for what He wishes.

His throne encompasses all of the heavens
and the Earth
and it is easy for Him
to preserve them.

He is the High, the Great.

Qu'ran 2:255 (7th century CE)

Maia Daguerre

Late have I loved you,
O Beauty ever ancient, ever new,
late have I loved you!

You were within me, but I was outside,
and it was there that I searched for you.

In my loveliness
I plunged into the lovely things
which you created.

You were with me, but I was not with you.

Created things kept me from you;
yet if they had not been in you
they would not have been at all.

You called, you shouted,
and you broke through my deafness.

You flashed, you shone,
and you dispelled my blindness.

You breathed your fragrance on me;
I drew in breath and now I pant for you.

I have tasted you,
now I hunger and thirst for more.

You touched me,
and I burned for your peace.

Saint Augustine (354–430)

Early Christian theologian and philosopher

Address to Supreme Deity

In heavens who is great? Thou alone art great!

On earth who is great? Thou alone art great!

When Thy voice resounds in heaven,
The gods fall prostrate!

When Thy voice resounds on earth,
The *genii* kiss the dust!

Assyrian Invocation

Kingdom of northern Mesopotamia (25th to 7th century BCE), located in what is now northern Iraq and southeastern Turkey.

"Genii" are supernatural creatures.

Maia Daguerre

The Lord's Prayer

Our Father in heaven,
may your name be kept holy.
Let your Kingdom come.
Let your will be done,
as in heaven, so on earth.
Give us today our daily bread.
Forgive us our debts,
as we also forgive our debtors.
Bring us not into temptation,
but deliver us from the evil one.
For yours is the Kingdom,
the power, and the glory forever.
Amen.

From the Gospel of Matthew 6:9–13 (1st century BCE)

Chapter III

GUIDANCE

Maia Daguerre

Lord, make me an instrument of Thy peace.
Where there is hatred, let me sow love;
Where there is injury, pardon;
Where there is doubt, faith;
Where there is despair, hope;
Where there is darkness, light;
Where there is sadness, joy.

O Divine Master,
Grant that I may not so much
Seek to be consoled as to console;
To be understood, as to understand;
To be loved, as to love.

For it is in giving that we receive;
It is in pardoning that we are pardoned;
It is in dying that we are born
To eternal life.

Attributed to Saint Francis of Assisi (1181/1182-1226)

According to modern scholars, the first appearance of this prayer occurred in France in 1912 in a small spiritual magazine called "La Clochette."

God's Aid

God to enfold me,
God to surround me,
God in my speaking,
God in my thinking.

God in my sleeping,
God in my waking,
God in my watching,
God in my hoping.

God in my life,
God in my lips,
God in my soul,
God in my heart.

God in my sufficing,
God in my slumber,
God in mine ever-living soul,
God in mine eternity.

Ancient Celtic Oral Tradition

Excerpt from the book "Carmina Gadelica" by Alexander Carmichael (1832–1912)

Maia Daguerre

Khatum

O Thou,
Who art the Perfection of Love, Harmony and Beauty,
The Lord of heaven and earth,
Open our hearts,
That we may hear Thy Voice,
Which constantly cometh from within.

Disclose to us Thy Divine Light,
Which is hidden in our souls,
That we may know
and understand Life better.

Most Merciful and Compassionate God,
Give us Thy great Goodness;
Teach us Thy loving Forgiveness;
Raise us above the distinctions
And differences that divide us;
Send us the Peace of Thy Divine Spirit,
And unite us all in Thy Perfect Being.

Amen.

Inayat Khan (1882 – 1927)
Indian musician, mystic philosopher and founder of the Sufi Movement

"Khātm" is a Hindustani word that means conclusion, seal, end.

O Great Spirit,

whose voice I hear in the winds and whose breath gives life to all the world, hear me.

I am small and weak. I need your strength and wisdom.

Let me walk in beauty, and make my eyes ever behold the red and purple sunset.

Make my hands respect the things you have made and my ears sharp to hear your voice.

Make me wise so that I may understand the things you have taught my people.

Let me learn the lessons you have hidden in every leaf and rock.

I seek strength, not to be superior to my brother, but to fight my greatest enemy: myself.

Make me always ready to come to you with clean hands and straight eyes.

So when life fades, as the fading sunset, my spirit will come to you without shame.

Lakota Chief Yellow Lark, 1887

Native American missionary and medicine man

Maia Daguerre

Serenity Prayer

God, give me grace to accept with serenity
To accept the things that cannot be changed.

Courage to change the things
Which should be changed.

And the wisdom to distinguish
The one from the other.

Living one day at a time; enjoying one moment at a time; accepting hardship as a pathway to peace; taking, as Jesus did, this sinful world as it is, not as I would have it.

Trusting that You will make all things right, if I surrender to Your will, so that I may be reasonably happy in this life and supremely happy with You forever in the next.

Amen.

Attributed to Reinhold Niebuhr (1892-1971)
American theologian

Salat al-Istikharah

O Allah!

I consult You as You are all Knowing, and I seek ability from Your power, and I ask you for Your great favor, for You have power, but I do not, and You have knowledge, but I do not, and You know all hidden matters.

O Allah! If You know that this matter is good for me in my religion, my livelihood and my life in the Hereafter, then make it easy and bless it;

And if You know that this matter is evil for me in my religion, my livelihood and my life in the Hereafter, then keep it away from me, and keep me away from it, and choose what is good for me, wherever it is, and make me pleased with it.

Traditional Islamic Prayer
Recited by Muslims when in need of guidance on an issue in their lives

Maia Daguerre

Grandfather,
Great Mysterious One,
You have been always and before You nothing has been.

There is nothing to pray to but You.

The star nations all over the universe are Yours,
and Yours are the grasses of the earth.

Day in and day out You are the life of things.

You are older than all need, older than all pain and prayer.

Grandfather,
all over the world, the faces of the living ones are alike.

In tenderness, they have come up out of the ground.

Look upon Your children
with children in their arms,
that they may face the winds,
and walk the good road to the day of quiet.

Teach me to walk the soft earth
like a relative to all that live.

Sweeten my heart and fill me with light,
and give me the strength to understand
and the eyes to see.

Help me, for without You I am nothing.

Black Elk (1863-1950)
Oglala Lakota medicine man

Although he converted to Roman Catholicism in later life, he continued to use the language of his ancestors to relate to God.

The Wesley Covenant Prayer

I am no longer my own, but yours.

Put me to what you will,
Rank me with whom you will;

Put me to doing,
Put me to suffering;

Let me be employed for you,
Or laid aside for you,
Exalted for you,
Or brought low for you;

Let me be full,
Let me be empty,
Let me have all things,
Let me have nothing:
I freely and wholeheartedly yield all things
To your pleasure and disposal.

And now,
Glorious and blessed God, Father, Son and Holy Spirit,
You are mine
and I am yours.

So be it.

And the covenant now made on earth,
Let it be ratified in heaven.

Amen.

Adapted by John Wesley (1703–1791)
Founder of Methodism

Maia Daguerre

God of our life,

there are days when the burdens we carry chafe our shoulders and weigh us down;

When the road seems dreary and endless,

The skies gray and threatening;

When our lives have no music in them, and our hearts are lonely, and our souls have lost their courage.

Flood the path with light, we beseech Thee;

Turn our eyes to where the skies are full of promise;

Tune our hearts to brave music;

Give us the sense of comradeship with heroes and saints of every age;

And so quicken our spirits, that we may be able to encourage the souls of all who journey with us on the road to life,

To Thy honor and glory.

Saint Augustine (354-430)

Early Christian theologian and philosopher whose writings influenced the development of Western Christianity and Western philosophy.

O Lord!

Make myself such
that I may have love for all beings,
joy in the meritorious,
unstinted sympathy for the distressed
and tolerance towards the perversely inclined.

O Lord!
May my soul always find fulfillment in friendship
and love towards all beings,
in all the virtuous,
in compassion toward all suffering creatures,
and in remaining neutral
towards those hostile to me.

This is my prayer.

Ancient Jain Prayer

One of the oldest religions in the world, Jainism prescribes a path of "ahimsa" (nonviolence) towards all living beings. The three main principles of Jainism are: Nonviolence ("Ahimsa"), Non-Absolutism ("Anekantavada") and Non-Possessiveness ("Aparigraha") and his followers take five major vows: non-violence, non-lying, non-stealing, non-attachment and chastity.

Maia Daguerre

Heavenly Father,
through your Eternal Word all of creation came into existence, and is held in being by your Holy Spirit. In the lives we lead and in the choices we make, help us to be mindful of the impact upon your world and its people, near and far, now and in future generations, so we may be faithful stewards of all that you have entrusted to us, until that time when all things are reconciled to you.

We pray for your wisdom, to safeguard the earth, its soil and all that grows in it. We pray for your understanding, to cleanse the air and all that breathes. We pray for your knowledge, to find ways to preserve our waters and all that live in them. We pray for your guidance, to protect all living beings with whom we share our planet. We pray for your compassion, to reach out to all those affected by extremes of weather, changes in climate, and the degradation of the environment.

We pray for your insight, to use the resources entrusted to us wisely and well, justly and safely. We pray for your perseverance, to ensure that all humanity may have adequate food and water, shelter and sanitation, peace and well-being, and so can live in dignity, without fear. We pray for your courage, to do all that is necessary to restore the beauty of your handiwork wherever we have damaged or harmed it. We pray for your grace, that each of us may be faithful stewards of all you have given us, in the choices we make and how we live our daily lives.

Creator and Redeemer, hear our prayer.

Gracious God, Creator and Redeemer of all that is, you have made human beings in your image and likeness, and by the work of your hands, fashioned the whole universe in beauty and majesty. Awaken in us a deeper reverence for all you have created, and renew among us eagerness to nurture and sustain your precious gift of life.

Amen.

Thabo Makgoba (1960-)
Anglican Archbishop of Cape Town, South Africa
Prayer written for The United Nations Conference on Sustainable Development (Rio+20) in Rio de Janeiro, Brazil, on 2012

Make Us Worthy

Make us worthy, Lord,
to serve our fellow men
throughout the world
who live and die
in poverty and hunger.

Give them
through our hands,
this day,
their daily bread,
and by our understanding love,
give peace and joy.

Pope Paul VI (1897-1978)

Maia Daguerre

Universal Prayer

We bow to the Goddess Mother Earth, who is the abode of bounteous blessings, the fulfiller of all needs and the ultimate refuge of all beings.

Our obeisance to the Almighty, who is the manifestation of truth, consciousness and bliss, and the only source of all universal well-being and Dharma.

O Lord, as we organize ourselves to stand united for the advancement of Universal Dharma, please bestow upon us your auspicious blessings so that we can accomplish this noble mission.

Grant us, O Lord of the universe, the invincible inner strength and virtuous character that all humanity adores, and the knowledge that will enlighten the path leading to our mission.

Let our hearts be always stimulated with that spirit of a solemn vow and determination of a hero, which will lead us to attain the worldly prosperity together with spiritual enhancement.

O Lord, give us that resolute faith in our aim to unite the people and establish world peace through propagation of Universal Dharma.

With your blessings, O Lord, let this triumphant Sangh strength attain the supreme external glory by protecting the principle of righteousness.

In this sacred work of serving and ennobling the entire humanity, give me the strength to accomplish it with single-minded focus and supreme sacrifice.

May this entire material and spiritual frame of mine be dedicated to this cause.

Traditional Hindu Prayer

Prayer to Our Lady of Guadalupe

Dear Mother, we love you.

We thank you for your promise to help us in our need.

We trust in your love that dries our tears and comforts us.

Teach us to find our peace in your Son, Jesus, and bless us every day of our lives.

Help us to build a shrine in our hearts.

Make it as beautiful as the one built for you on the *Mount of Tepeyac*.

A shrine full of trust, hope, and love of Jesus growing stronger each day.

Mary, you have chosen to remain with us by giving us your most wonderful and holy self-image on *Juan Diego's cloak*.

May we feel your loving presence as we look upon your face.

Like Juan, give us the courage to bring your message of hope to everyone.

You are our Mother and our inspiration.

Hear our prayers and answer us.

Amen.

Traditional Catholic Prayer
Mount of Tepeyac, in Mexico, had been a place for worshipping Aztec earth goddesses. According to the Catholic tradition, it is the site where, in December of 1531, Saint Juan Diego met the Virgin of Guadalupe and received her iconic image.

Maia Daguerre

Lord, teach me to pray.
It sounds exciting, put like that.
It sounds real. An exploration.
A chance to do more than catalogue
and list the things I want,
to an eternal Father Christmas.
The chance of meeting you,
of drawing closer to the love that made me,
and keeps me, and knows me.
And, Lord, it's only just begun.
There is so much more of you,
of love, the limitless expanse of knowing you.
I could be frightened, Lord, in this wide country.
It could be lonely, but you are here, with me.
The chance of learning about myself,
of facing up to what I am.
Admitting my resentments,
bringing my anger to you,
my disappointments, my frustration.
And finding that when l do,
when I stop struggling and shouting
and let go you are still there. Still loving.
Sometimes, Lord, often –
I don't know what to say to you.
But I still come, in quiet
for the comfort of two friends
sitting in silence.
And it's then, Lord, that I learn most from you.
When my mind slows down,
and my heart stops racing.
When I let go and wait in the quiet,
realizing that all the things I was going to ask for
you know already.
Then, Lord, without words, in the stillness
you are there...
And l love you.
Lord, teach me to pray.

Eddie Askew (1927-2007)
English artist and writer

From the book "A silence and a shouting"

I cannot dance, O Lord,
Unless You lead me.

If You wish me to leap joyfully,
Let me see You dance.

Let me see You dance joyfully.
Let me see You dance and sing.

Then I will leap into Love
And from Love into Knowledge,
From Knowledge into the Harvest,
That sweetest fruit beyond human sense.

There I will stay with you,
Whirling.

Mechtild of Magdeburg (1210 –1280)

Medieval mystic

Maia Daguerre

Lead me from the unreal
to the real;
from darkness to light;
and from death to immortality.

Traditional Hindu Prayer

I am of the nature to grow old.

There is no way to escape growing old.

I am of the nature to have ill-health.
There is no way to escape having ill-health.

I am of the nature to die.
There is no way to escape death.

All that is dear to me and everyone I love
Are of the nature to change.

There is no way to escape being separated from them.

My actions are my only true belongings.

I cannot escape the consequences of my actions.

My actions are the ground on which I stand.

Buddha (6th / 4th century BCE)

Chapter IV

FORGIVENESS

Forgive me, O Lord;
Forgive me, O holy Mother of God;
Forgive me, O ye Angels,
Archangels, Cherubim and Seraphim,
and all ye heavenly host!

Forgive, O sky;
Forgive, O damp-mother-earth;
Forgive, O sun;
Forgive, O moon;
Forgive, ye stars;
Forgive, ye lakes, ye rivers and hills;
Forgive, all ye heavenly and earthly elements.

Ancient Russian Prayer

From "Songs of the Russian People" by W. R. S. Ralston (1872)

Maia Daguerre

Lesson 122
Forgiveness offers everything I want.

What could you want forgiveness cannot give? Do you want peace? Forgiveness offers it. Do you want happiness, a quiet mind, a certainty of purpose, and a sense of worth and beauty that transcends the world? Do you want care and safety, and the warmth of sure protection always? Do you want a quietness that cannot be disturbed, a gentleness that never can be hurt, a deep, abiding comfort, and a rest so perfect it can never be upset?

Forgiveness offers everything I want. Today I have accepted this as true. Today I have received the gifts of God.

Helen Schucman (1909 –1981)
American Clinical and Research Psychologist

From the book "A Course in Miracles" channeled from 1975 to 1962. The author believed that an "inner voice," which she identified as Jesus, guided her writing.

Father, Forgive them;
For they don't know what they are doing.

From the Gospel of Luke 23:34 (1st century CE)

Maia Daguerre

To recite after Salat Alan-Nabi:

O Lord,
make me and my children
keep up prayers.

Our Lord,
accept our prayer.

Our Lord,
forgive me and my parents
and all the Believers
on the Day of Judgment.

Traditional Islamic Prayer

"Salat Alan-Nabi" (Darud) means "Salutation to the Prophet"

Prayer for Repentance

All that I ought to have thought and have not thought,
All that I ought to have said and have not said,
All that I ought to have done and have not done,
All that I ought to have ordered and have not ordered,
All that I ought not to have thought and yet have thought,
All that I ought not to have spoken and yet have spoken,
All that I ought not to have done and yet have done,
All that I ought not to have ordered and yet have ordered;

For thoughts, words, and works,
Bodily and spiritual,
Earthy and heavenly,
Pray I for forgiveness,
And repent of it with penance.

Zoroastrian Prayer (2nd millennium BCE)
From the book "The Teachings of Zoroaster" by S. A. Kapadia (1905)

Zoroastrianism is one of the world's oldest religions that arose in the eastern region of the ancient Persian Empire and influenced other later religions including Judaism, Gnosticism, Christianity and Islam.

Maia Daguerre

Forgive me, most gracious Lord and Father,
if this day I have done or said anything to increase the pain of the world.

Pardon the unkind word, the impatient gesture, the hard and selfish deed, the failure to show sympathy, and kindly help where I had the opportunity, but missed it;

And enable me so to live that I may daily do something to lessen the tide of human sorrow, and add to the sum of human happiness.

Unknown Author

Forgiveness

Praise be unto Thee, O Lord.

Forgive us our sins, have mercy upon us and enable us to return unto Thee.

Suffer us not to rely on aught else besides Thee, and vouchsafe unto us, through Thy bounty, that which Thou lovest and desirest and well beseemeth Thee.

Exalt the station of them that have truly believed, and forgive them with Thy gracious forgiveness.

Verily, Thou art the Help in Peril, the Self-Subsisting.

The Báb (1819 –1850)
Founder of Bábism and one central figure of the Bahá'í Faith

Maia Daguerre

Forgiving Father, forgive us for our sins.

Forgive us for repeating patterns of financial failures such as living beyond our means and misusing credit cards.

Forgive those in our congregation and our communities for a heavy dependence on payday loans and pawn shops.

Forgive us for failing to develop financial plans that include debt reduction, savings and investments.

Forgive those of us who believe that we are supposed to have the most of the worst and the least of the best.

Forgive those in our congregation who have contributed to poverty-like conditions for many of our children by refusing to make court-ordered child support payments.

Lord, forgive me for *(list any sins that you have committed)*.

Holy Spirit, remind us all of those we need to forgive and help us to be quick to forgive.

(Take a moment and ask the Holy Spirit to show you names or faces of people that you may need to forgive. As He shows you, say aloud, "I forgive (name of person(s)."

Now, trust the Lord to heal any wounds in your soul caused by unforgiveness).

Pastor Suzette Caldwell (1962-) / The Prayer Institute
American Pastor

Forgiveness

O Lord, remember not only the men
and woman of good will, but also those of ill will.

But do not remember all of the suffering they have inflicted upon us:

Instead remember the fruits we have borne because of this suffering — our fellowship, our loyalty to one another, our humility, our courage, our generosity, the greatness of heart that has grown from this trouble.

When our persecutors come to be judged by you, let all of these fruits that we have borne be their forgiveness.

Found in the clothing of a dead child at Ravensbruck concentration camp (1945)

Maia Daguerre

The Litany of Reconciliation

The hatred which divides nation from nation, race from race, class from class,
Father, forgive.

The covetous desires of people and nations to possess what is not their own,
Father, forgive.

The greed which exploits the work of human hands and lays waste the earth,
Father forgive.

Our envy of the welfare and happiness of others.
Father forgive.

Our indifference to the plight of the imprisoned, the homeless, the refugee.
Father, forgive.

The lust which dishonors the bodies of men, women, and children,
Father, forgive.

The pride which leads us to trust in ourselves and not in God,
Father, forgive.

Be kind to one another, tenderhearted, forgiving one another, as God in Christ forgave you.

Coventry Cathedral Prayer (1958)

Following the bombing of the medieval cathedral in 1940 by the Nazis, Provost Richard Howard had the words "Father Forgive" inscribed on the wall behind the altar of the ruined building.

The Litany of Reconciliation is prayed in the new Cathedral every weekday at noon (in the Ruins on Fridays) and is used throughout the world by the Community of the Cross of Nails

O God, forgive the poverty,

the pettiness, Lord, the childish folly of our prayers.

Listen, not to our words, but to the groanings that cannot be uttered; hearken, not to our petitions, but to the crying of our need.

So often we pray for that which is already ours, neglected and unappropriated;

so often for that which never can be ours; so often for that which we must win ourselves; and then labor endlessly for that which can only come to us in prayer.

How often we have prayed for the coming of thy kingdom, yet when it has sought to come through us we have sometimes barred the way; we have wanted it without in others, but not in our own hearts.

We feel it is we who stand between man's need and thee; between ourselves and what we might be; and we have no trust in our own strength, or loyalty, or courage.

O give us to love thy ill, and seek thy kingdom first of all.

Sweep away our fears, our compromise, our weakness, lest at last we be found fighting against thee.

Amen.

William E Orchard (1877-1955)
Liturgist, Pacifist and Ecumenicist

Maia Daguerre

Our Lord, do not mind us
if we forget or make mistakes;

Our Lord, do not place a burden upon us as You have placed upon those before us;

Our Lord, do not place upon us what we cannot bare;

Pardon us, and forgive us, and have mercy on us;

You are our patron, grant us victory over the disbelieving people.

Qu'ran 2:286 (7th century CE)

Ho'oponopono Mantra

I'm Sorry.

Please forgive me.

I love you.

Thank you.

"Ho'oponopono" is an ancient Hawaiian practice of reconciliation and forgiveness

Chapter V

AWAKENING

Bodhisattva Prayer for Humanity

May I be a guard
For those who need protection,
A guide for those on the path,
A boat, a raft, a bridge
For those who wish to cross the flood.

May I be a lamp in the darkness,
A resting place for the weary,
A healing medicine
For all who are sick,
A vase of plenty,
A tree of miracles;

And for the boundless multitudes
Of living beings
May I bring sustenance and awakening
Enduring like the earth and sky
Until all beings are freed from sorrow
And all are awakened.

Shantideva (8th century CE)
Indian Buddhist Monk

Prayer performed each morning by His Holiness the Dalai Lama

In Buddhism, a bodhisattva is an enlightened (bodhi) being (sattva).

Maia Daguerre

May I be at peace.

May my heart remain open.

May I be aware of my true nature.

May I be healed.

May I be a source of healing to others.

May I dwell in the Breath of God.

Saint Teresa of Avila (1515–1582)

Spanish Mystic, Roman Catholic Saint and Founder of the Discalced Carmelites

Looking behind, I am filled with gratitude.
Looking forward, I am filled with vision.
Looking upwards, I am filled with strength.
Looking within, I discover peace.

Unknown Author

Maia Daguerre

Nirvanashatkam

I am not mind, nor intellect, nor ego, nor the reflections of inner self.
I am not the five senses.
I am beyond that.
I am not the ether, nor the earth, nor the fire, nor the wind.
I am indeed, that eternal knowing and bliss, the auspicious, love and pure consciousness.

Neither can I be termed as energy, nor five types of breath, nor the seven material essences, nor the five sheaths.
Neither am I the five instruments of elimination, procreation, motion, grasping, or speaking.
I am indeed, that eternal knowing and bliss, the auspicious, love and pure consciousness.

I have no hatred or dislike, nor affiliation or liking, nor greed, nor delusion, nor pride or haughtiness, nor feelings of envy or jealousy.
I have no duty, nor any money, nor any desire, nor even liberation.
I am indeed, that eternal knowing and bliss, the auspicious, love and pure consciousness.

I have neither merit, nor demerit.
I do not commit sins or good deeds, nor have happiness or sorrow, pain or pleasure.
I do not need mantras, holy places, scriptures, rituals or sacrifices.
I am none of the triad of the observer or one who experiences, the process of observing or experiencing, or any object being observed or experienced.
I am indeed, that eternal knowing and bliss, the auspicious, love and pure consciousness.

I do not have fear of death, as I do not have death.
I have no separation from my true self, no doubt about my existence, nor have I discrimination on the basis of birth.
I have no father or mother, nor did I have a birth.
I am not the relative, nor the friend, nor the guru, nor the disciple.

I am indeed, that eternal knowing and bliss, the auspicious, love and pure consciousness.

I am all-pervasive. I am without any attributes, and without any form.
I have neither attachment to the world, nor to liberation.
I have no wishes for anything because I am everything, everywhere, every time, always in equilibrium.
I am indeed, that eternal knowing and bliss, the auspicious, love and pure consciousness.

Traditional Hindu Prayer attributed to Adi Shankara (788-820 CE)

"Nirvanashatkam," known as "The Song of The Self" is a composition consisting of the teachings of the Advaita Vedanta (Non-Dualistic Philosophy), practiced by Yogis.

Maia Daguerre

Song of Vibhuti Yoga

I am neither mind nor body, immortal self I am,
I am witness of three states, I am knowledge absolute.

I am fragrance in Jessamine, beauty in flowers,
I am coolness in the ice, flavor in coffee.

I am greenness in the leaf, hue in the rainbow,
I am taste-buds in the tongue, essence in orange.

I am mind of all minds, prana of all pranas,
I am soul of souls, self of all selves.

I am Atman in all beings, apple of all eyes,
I am sun of all suns, light of all lights.

I am pranava of all Vedas, Brahman of Upanishads,
I am silence in forests, thunder in all clouds.

I am velocity in electrons, motion in science,
I am effulgence in the sun, wave in the radio.

I am support of this world, soul of this body,
I am ear of all ears, eye of all eyes.

I am time, space, and the controller,
I am god of gods, guru and the director.

I am melody in music, in rag and raginins,
I am sound in ether, Shakti in Virya.

I am power in electricity, intelligence in mind,
I am brilliance in fire, penance in ascetics.

I am reason in philosopher, will in Jnanis,
I am Prem in Bhaktas, Samadhi in Yogis.

I am that I am, I am that I am, I am that I am, I am that I am.

Swami Sivananda (1887–1963)
Hindu Spiritual Teacher and Yoga Master

Sanskrit dictionaries define "vibhuti" as "manifestations of divine power." In some versions of "The Bhagavad Gita", the title of Chapter Ten, "The Yoga of Vibhuti," is translated as "Manifestations of the Power and Glory of God."

Contemplation on No-Coming and No-Going

This body is not me.

I am not limited by this body.

I am life without boundaries.

I have never been born and I have never died.

Look at the ocean and the sky filled with stars,

manifestations from my wondrous true mind.

Since before time I have been free.

Birth and death are only doors through which we pass,

sacred thresholds on our journey.

Birth and death are a game of hide-and-seek.

So laugh with me, hold my hand, let us say good-bye,

say good-bye,

to meet again soon.

We meet today.

We will meet again tomorrow.

We will meet at the source every moment.

We meet each other in all forms of life.

Thich Nhat Hanh (1926-)
Vietnamese Zen Buddhist Monk, Teacher, Author, Poet and Peace Activist

From the book "Chanting From the Heart"

Maia Daguerre

Oracle of Sumiyoshi (Prayer of Benevolence)

I have no corporeal existence,
but Universal Benevolence is my divine body.

I have no physical power,
but uprightness is my strength.

I have no religious clairvoyance,
beyond what is bestowed by wisdom.

I have no power of miracle,
other than the attainment of quiet happiness.

I have no tact
except the exercise of gentleness.

Traditional Shinto Prayer (7th century BCE)

Shinto is the indigenous tradition of Japan. Their followers observe ancient practices of ritual purification, nature worship, and abstinence to honor the "kami" (divine spirits). Shinto is unique among religions because there are no founders, no written scriptures, and no required form of worship. Most remarkable, its believers are encouraged to practice Shinto in combination with other religions.

I see no stranger, I see no enemy
Wherever I look, God is all I see.

I don't think of us and them
No one do I hate or condemn
I see God's image – each one a friend.

Of any religion, caste or race
All I see is God's shining face
His smiling face,
His gracious face.

Accept as beautiful all His design
I learnt this truth in sangat divine.

One Word resounds in me and you
Waheguru ... Waheguru ...

In him, in her, in me and you
Waheguru ... Waheguru ...

Beholding in every being His light
I bloom like a flower in joy and delight.

Guru Arjan (1563–1606)
Excerpt from "The Adi Granth" translated by Dr. Inder Mohan Singh

"The Adi Granth" is the sacred scripture of Sikhism, a monotheistic religion founded during the 15th century in the Punjab region of South Asia. The book is the central object of worship in all temples and is revered as a living Guru. "Waheguru" means "wonderful teacher" in the Punjabi language, and is used to refer to God.

Maia Daguerre

Be generous in prosperity,
and thankful in adversity.

Be worthy of the trust of thy neighbor, and look upon him with a bright and friendly face.

Be a treasure to the poor, an admonisher to the rich, an answerer of the cry of the needy, a preserver of the sanctity of thy pledge.

Be fair in thy judgment, and guarded in thy speech.

Be unjust to no man, and show all meekness to all men.

Be as a lamp unto those who walk in darkness, a joy to the sorrowful, a sea for the thirsty, a haven for the distressed, an upholder and defender of the victim of oppression.

Let integrity and uprightness distinguish all thine acts.

Be a home for the stranger, a balm to the suffering, a tower of strength for the fugitive.

Be eyes to the blind, and a guiding light unto the feet of the erring.

Be an ornament to the countenance of truth, a crown to the brow of fidelity, a pillar of the temple of righteousness, a breath of life to the body of mankind, an ensign of the hosts of justice, a luminary above the horizon of virtue, a dew to the soil of the human heart, an ark on the ocean of knowledge, a sun in the heaven of bounty, a gem on the diadem of wisdom, a shining light in the firmament of thy generation, a fruit upon the tree of humility.

Bá'u'lláh (1817–1892)
Founder of the Bahá'í Faith

Monotheistic religion that emphasizes the spiritual unity of all humankind.

First I Thank the Source of All Life
for this life's meaning.

Then I can begin.

First I create the space
in which to grow into new dimensions.

Then I can move there.

First I envision the garden full of rainbows
and scents of nectar.

Then I can plan them.

First I touch my heartstring and feel its resonance
with the harmonics of all beings.

Then I can share love.

First I hear the bird sing
filling the garden with melodies beyond my ears.

Then I can appreciate Life's music.

First I taste the morning light
with which to create food for my soul.

Then I can cook.

Harriet Kofalk (1937-1996)
American Naturalist, Author, Activist and Teacher

Maia Daguerre

Golden Chain

I am a link in Amida Buddha's golden chain of love that stretches around the world.

In gratitude, may I keep my link bright and strong.

I will try to be kind and gentle to every living thing, and protect all who are weaker than myself.

I will try to think pure and beautiful thoughts, to say pure and beautiful words, and to do pure and beautiful deeds.

May every link in Amida Buddha's golden chain of love be bright and strong, and may we all attain perfect peace.

Traditional Shin Buddhist Prayer

"Amida Buddha" is the Japanese translation of the Sanskrit Indian "Amitabha." It is translatable as "Infinite Light," hence "Amitabha" is often called "The Buddha of Infinite Light."

And I think over again
My small adventures
When from a shore wind
I drifted out in my kayak
And I thought I was in danger.

My fears
Those small ones
That I thought so big
For all the vital things
I had to get and to reach.

And yet, there is only one great thing
The only thing.

To live and see in huts and on journeys
The great day that dawns
And the light that fills the world.

Inuit Song

Indigenous peoples inhabiting the Arctic regions of Greenland, Canada, and Alaska

O cosmic power!
Ignite our spirits for purposeful mission;
Inject positive energy in our brains;
Transmit divine virtues in our attitudes;
Transform inner self on the path of Self–Enlightenment.

O Infinite Intelligence!
Supercharge the light of knowledge in our hearts;
Circulate the wave of creativity in our minds;
Stabilize thy adorable glory in our consciousnesses;
Spread thy glorious radiance on our bodies.

O Super Consciousness!
Pour purity of knowledge in our thoughts;
Lead our deeds towards self- realization;
Equalize our frequencies of souls with thy super soul,
for attaining perfect condition of Resonance-Bliss.

O eternal love!
Inspire us for structuring an architect of character;
Supercharge high intensive love in our all actions;
Illuminate our life with glare, grace and grandeur;
Generate rays of happiness in our family matrix.

Traditional Hindu Prayer

Birth is a beginning and death a destination:
From childhood to maturity and youth to age;
From innocence to awareness and ignorance to knowing;
From foolishness to discretion and then, perhaps to wisdom;
From weakness to strength or strength to weakness, and back again;
From health to sickness and back to health again;
From offense to forgiveness;
From loneliness to love;
From joy to gratitude;
From pain to compassion;
From grief to understanding;
From fear to faith;
From defeat to defeat until looking backward or ahead,
we see that victory lies not at some high place along the way,
but in having made the journey stage by stage a sacred pilgrimage.

Birth is a beginning and death a destination,
and life is a journey;

A sacred journey to life everlasting.

Traditional Yom Kippur Prayer

Maia Daguerre

Prayer when opening a door

I pray thee, Lord, to open the door of my heart to receive thee within my heart.

When washing clothes

I pray thee, Lord, to wash my heart, making me white as snow.

When sweeping floors

I pray thee, Lord, to sweep away my heart's uncleanness, that my heart may always be pure.

When pouring oil

I pray thee, Lord, to give me wisdom like the wise virgins who always had oil in their vessels.

When posting a letter

I pray thee, Lord, to add to me faith upon faith, that I may always have communication with thee.

When lighting lamps

I pray thee, Lord, to make my deeds excellent like lamps before others, and more, to place thy light within my heart.

When watering flowers

I pray thee, Lord, to send down spiritual rain into my heart to germinate the good seed there.

When boiling water for tea

I pray thee, Lord, to send down spiritual fire to burn away the coldness of my heart and that I may always be hot-hearted in serving thee.

Prayer by Chinese Christian Women

Prayer on building a wall

I pray to thee, Lord, to make my faith as firmly established as a house built upon a rock, so that neither rain, flood nor wind can ever destroy it.

On pruning a tree

I pray to thee, Lord, to purge me and take away my selfishness and sinful thoughts, that I may bring forth more fruits of the Spirit.

On tending sheep

I pray to thee, Lord, to protect me from evil and keep me from want, daily carrying me in thine arms like a lamb.

On winnowing grain

I pray to thee, Lord, to winnow away the chaff from my heart and make it like the true wheat, for to be garnered in thy barn.

On sowing seed

I pray to thee, Lord, to sow the good seed of virtue in my heart, letting it grow by day and night and bring forth a hundredfold.

On writing a book

I pray to thee, Lord, by the precious blood of Jesus, to pay my debt of sin and write my name in heaven, making me free in body and soul.

On planing wood

I pray to thee, Lord, to make me smooth and straight, fit to be a useful vessel, pleasing to the Lord.

On drawing water

I pray to thee, Lord, to give living water to quench my thirst, and wash away the stains from my heart.

Prayer by Chinese Christian Men

Maia Daguerre

O lord my God,
I see you at the gate of paradise,
and I do not know what I see,
for I see nothing visible.

The only thing I know
is that I do not know what I see
and can never know.

You are infinity,
and can only be approached
by those who understand
that they do not know you at all.

Nicholas de Cusa (1400 – 1464)
German Philosopher, Mystic and Astronomer

O Jesus, my feet are dirty.

Come even as a slave to me, pour water into your bowl, come and wash my feet.

In asking such a thing I know I am overbold but I dread what was threatened when you said to me:

"If I do not wash your feet I have no fellowship with you."

Wash my feet then, because I long for your companionship.

And yet, what am I asking?

It was well for Peter to ask you to wash his feet, for him that was all that was needed for him to be clean in every part.

With me it is different: though you wash me now I shall still stand in need of that other washing, the cleansing you promised when you said:

"There is a baptism I must needs be baptized with."

Origen of Alexandria (185–254)
Scholar and Early Christian Theologian

Maia Daguerre

That is perfect.
This is perfect.
Out of perfect only perfect comes.
Even after taking perfect out of perfect,
that is perfect which remains.
All this whatsoever moves in this universe
including the universe, itself moving,
is indwelt or pervaded or enveloped or clothed by the Lord.
That renounced, thou shouldst enjoy.
Covet not any body's wealth.

Excerpt from Hindu Scriptures

A Warrior's Creed

I have no parents:
I make the heaven and earth my parents.

I have no home:
I make awareness my home.

I have no life and death:
I make the tides of breathing my life and death.

I have no divine powers:
I make honesty my divine power.

I have no means:
I make understanding my means.

I have no secrets:
I make character my secret.

I have no body:
I make endurance my body.

I have no eyes:
I make the flash of lightening my eyes.

I have no ears:
I make sensibility my ears.

I have no limbs:
I make promptness my limbs.

I have no strategy:
I make "unshadowed by thought" my strategy.

I have no design:
I make "seizing opportunity by the forelock" my design.

I have no miracles:
I make right action my miracle.

I have no principles:
I make adaptability to all circumstances my principle.

Maia Daguerre

I have no tactics:
I make emptiness and fullness my tactics.

I have no talent:
I make ready wit my talent.

I have no friends:
I make my mind my friend.

I have no enemy:
I make carelessness my enemy.

I have no armor:
I make benevolence and righteousness my armor.

I have no castle:
I make immovable mind my castle.

I have no sword:
I make absence of self my sword.

Anonymous Samurai Song (14th century)

Chapter VI

MOTHER EARTH

Maia Daguerre

Hymn to The All-Mother

Hail to our Mother who makes the yellow flowers to bloom - who scatters the seeds of the maguey as she comes from the Land Divine!

Hail to our Mother who casts forth white flowers in abundance!

Hail to our Mother who shines in the thorn bush as a bright butterfly!

Ho! She is our Mother - the woman god of the earth. In the desert she feeds the wild beasts, and gives them to live.

Thus - thus you see her ever abundant in gifts to all flesh.

And as you see the goddess of earth give to the beasts, so also she is giving to the green herbs and the fishes.

Hail to our Mother who casts forth yellow flowers to the sun from the Land Divine!

Ancient Mexican Hymn

Hymn dedicated to the goddess Teteoinan, the "Mother of Gods", also known by another name meaning "Heart of the Earth." Her chief temple was on the spot selected by the early missionaries for the "Lady of Guadalupe" to make her appearance, and the native shrine was razed to make way for the temple of the imported cult of Christendom.

From "Pagan Prayers" by Marah Ellis Ryan (1913)

Four Directions Prayer

Creator, it is I.

Thank you for today's sunrise, for the breath and life within me, and for all of your creations.

Creator, hear my prayer, and honor my prayer. As the day begins with the rising sun, I ask:

Spirit keeper of the East, Brother Eagle, be with me. Fly high as you carry my prayers to the Creator.

May I have eyes as sharp as yours, so I am able to see truth and hope on the path I have chosen.

Guide my step and give me courage to walk the circle of my life with honesty and dignity.

Spirit keeper of the South, Wolf, be with me. Help me to remember to love and feel compassion for all mankind.

Help me to walk my path with joy and love for myself, for others, for the four legged, the winged ones, the plants and all creation upon Mother Earth.

Show me it is right for me to make decisions with my heart, even if at times, my heart becomes hurt.

Help me to grow and nurture my self-worth in all ways.

Spirit Keeper of the West, Brown Bear, be with me. Bring healing to the people I love and to myself.

Bring into balance the physical, mental and spiritual, so I am able to know my place on this earth, in life and in death.

Heal my body, heal my mind and bring light, joy and awareness to my spirit.

Spirit Keeper of the North, White Buffalo, be with me.

As each day passes, help me to surrender, with grace, the things of my youth.

Help me to listen to the quiet, and find serenity and comfort in the silences as they become longer.

Give me wisdom so I am able to make wise choices in all things which are put in front of me.

And when time for my change of worlds has come, let me go peacefully, without regrets for the things I neglected to do as I walked along my path.

Mother Earth, thank you for your beauty, and for all you have given me.

Remind me never to take from you more then I need, and remind me to always give back more than I take.

Vera Dery (2002)
From http://www.highonlife1.com

Sláva

Glory to God in Heaven, *Glory*!
To our Lord on this Earth, *Glory*!
May our Lord never grow old, *Glory*!
May his bright robes never be spoiled, *Glory*!
May his good steeds never be worn out, *Glory*!
May his trusty servants never falter, *Glory*!
May the Right throughout Russia, *Glory*!
Be fairer than the bright Sun, *Glory*!
May the Tsar's golden treasury, *Glory*!
Be forever full to the brim, *Glory*!
May the great rivers, *Glory*!
Bear their renown to the sea, *Glory*!
The little streams to the mill, *Glory*!
But this song we sing to the Corn, *Glory*!
To the Corn we sing, the Corn we honor, *Glory*!
For the old folks to enjoy, *Glory*!
For the good folks to hear, *Glory!*

Traditional Russian Song
From "Songs of the Russian People" by W. R. S. Ralston (1872)

"Sláva" means "Glory"

Maia Daguerre

Though my heart desires shield flowers,

Life Giver's flowers, what might happen to this heart of mine? Alas, it's for nothing that we've come to be born here on earth.

I'm to pass away like a ruined flower. My fame will be nothing, my renown here on earth will be nothing. There may be flowers, there may be songs, but what might happen to this heart of mine? Alas, it's for nothing that we've come to be born here on earth.

Friends, be pleasured! Let us put our arms round each other's shoulders here. We're living in a world of flowers here. No one when he's gone can enjoy the flowers, the songs that lie outspread in this home of Life Giver.

Earth is but a moment. Is the Place Unknown the same? Is there happiness and friendship? Is it not just here on earth that friends are made?

Ancient Aztec Poem (14th / 16th century CE)

Excerpt from the book "Cantares Mexicanos: Songs of the Aztecs" translated by John Bierhorst

O our Father, the Sky,
hear us and make us strong.

O our Mother, the Earth, hear us and give us support.

O Spirit of the East, send us your Wisdom.

O Spirit of the South, may we tread your path.

O Spirit of the West, may we always be ready for the long journey.

O Spirit of the North, purify us with your cleansing winds.

Sioux Prayer
Native American Indigenous People

Maia Daguerre

The Canticle of the Creatures

Most High, all-powerful, all-good Lord,
All praise is Yours, all glory, honor and blessings.
To you alone, Most High, do they belong,
No mortal lips are worthy to pronounce Your Name.
We praise You, Lord, for all Your creatures,
Especially for Brother Sun,
Who is the day through whom You give us light.
And he is beautiful and radiant with great splendor,
Of You Most High, he bears your likeness.
We praise You, Lord, for Sister Moon and the stars,
In the heavens you have made them bright, precious and fair.
We praise You, Lord, for Brothers Wind and Air,
Fair and stormy, all weather's moods,
By which You cherish all that You have made.
We praise You, Lord, for Sister Water,
So useful, humble, precious and pure.
We praise You, Lord, for Brother Fire,
Through whom You light the night.
He is beautiful, playful, robust, and strong.
We praise You, Lord, for Sister Earth,
Who sustains us with her fruits, colored flowers, and herbs.
We praise You, Lord, for those who pardon,
For love of You bear sickness and trial.
Blessed are those who endure in peace,
By You Most High, they will be crowned.
We praise You, Lord, for Sister Death,
From whom no-one living can escape.
Woe to those who die in their sins!
Blessed are those that She finds doing Your Will.
No second death can do them harm.
We praise and bless You, Lord, and give You thanks,
And serve You in all humility.
Saint Francis of Assisi (1181/1182-1226)

May all I say
and all I think
be in harmony with Thee,
God within me,
God beyond me,
maker of the trees.

Chinook Prayer
Native American Indigenous People

Maia Daguerre

O Lord, O God, Creator of our land,

our earth, the trees, the animals and humans, all is for your honor.

The drums beat it out, and people sing about it, and they dance with noisy joy that you are The Lord.

You also have pulled the continents out of the sea.

What a wonderful world you have made, out of the wet mud, and what beautiful men and women!

We thank you for the beauty of this earth.

The grace of your creation is like a cool day between rainy seasons.

We drink in your creation with our eyes.

We listen to the birds and everything that grows there.

The sky above us is like a warm, soft Kente cloth, because you are behind it, else it would be cold and rough and uncomfortable.

We drink in your creation and cannot get enough of it.

But in doing we forget the evil we have done, Lord, we call to you, we beg you, tear us away from our sins and our death as this wonderful world fades away.

And one day our eyes snap shut, and all is over and dead that is not from you.

We are still slaves of the fetishes of this earth, when we are not saved by you.

Bless us, bless our land and people, bless our forests with mahogany, wawo and cacao.

Bless our fields with cassava and peanuts.

Bless our waters that flow through our land.

Fill them with fish and drive great schools of fish to our seacoast, so that our fishermen in their unsteady boats do not go out too far.

Be with us in our country, and in all Africa, and in the whole world.

Prepare us for the service that we should render.

Ashanti Prayer
Nation and Ethnic Group Native of South Ghana, Africa

Dadirri is deep listening.
Listening to the land.
Listening to the spirit speaking through the land.
Listening to the stillness.

Dadirri is awareness of the land
as sacred Silent awareness
of deep springs within me.

I am the story of the land.
I feel the harmony that is in the land.
My life is sacred.
A deep theme unfolding.

Dadirri makes me feel whole.
Renews me and brings peace.

My life is new.

Australian Aboriginal Prayer
"Dadirri" means "deep listening" and it is used as spiritual practice

Maia Daguerre

Grandfather, Great Spirit,
once more behold me on earth and lean to hear my feeble voice.

You lived first, and you are older than all need, older than all prayer.

All things belong to you – the two-legged, the four- legged, the wings of the air, and all green things that live.

You have set the powers of the four quarters of the earth to cross each other.

You have made me cross the good road and road of difficulties, and where they cross, the place is holy.

Day in, day out, forever more, you are the life of things.

Hey! Lean to hear my feeble voice.

At the center of the sacred hoop, you have said that I should make the tree to bloom.

With tears running, O Great Spirit, my Grandfather, with running eyes, I must say: the tree has never bloomed.

Here I stand, and the tree is withered.

Again, I recall the great vision you gave me.

It may be that some little root of the sacred tree still lives.

Nourish it then, that it may leaf and bloom, and fill with singing birds!

Hear me, that the people may once again find the good road and the shielding tree.

Black Elk (1863-1950)
Oglala Lakota medicine man

Although he converted to Roman Catholicism in later life, he continued to use the language of his ancestors to relate to God.

The mountains, I become a part of it...

The herbs, the fir tree, I become a part of it...
The morning mists, the clouds,
the gathering waters, I become a part of it...
The wilderness, the dew drops, the pollen...
I become a part of it...

Navajo Chant
Native American Indigenous People

Maia Daguerre

Invocation to The *U'wannami*

Come you, ascend the ladder; all come in; all sit down.
We were poor, poor, poor, poor, poor, poor,
When we came to this world through the poor place,
Where the body of water dried for our passing.
Banked up clouds cover the earth.
All come four times with your showers,
Descend to the base of the ladder and stand still;
Bring your showers and great rains.
All, all come, all ascend, all come in, all sit down.

I throw out to you my sacred meal that you may all come.
Hold your gaming-stick; throw it forward; all come.
All come out and give us your showers and great rains; all come,
That the seeds may be strong and come up, that all seed plants may come up and be strong.
Come you that all trees and seeds may come up and be strong.
Come you hither; all come.

Cover my earth mother four times with many flowers.
Let the heavens be covered with the banked-up clouds.
Let the earth be covered with fog; cover the earth with rains.
Great waters, rains, cover the earth.
Lighting cover the earth.
Let thunder be heard over the earth;
let thunder be heard;
Let thunder be heard
over the six regions of the earth.

Zuni Prayer for Rain
Native American indigenous people

From the book "The Path on the Rainbow: An Anthology of Songs and Chants from the Indians of North America" edited by George W. Cronyn (1918)

"U'wannami" is the rain-maker deity to whom the rain-priest and his assistants sing all night long and to whom they offer their fetishes.

The Prayer for the Earth

We gently caress you, the Earth, our planet and our home.

Our vision has brought us closer to you, making us aware of the harm we have done to the life-network upon which we ourselves depend.

We are reminded that we have poisoned your waters, your lands, your air.

We have filled you with the bones of our dead from war and greed.

Your pain is our pain.

Touching you gently, we pray that we may become peace-bringers and life-bringers, so that our home in its journey around the Sun not become a sterile and lonely place.

May this prayer and its power last forever.

Sensei Fredrich Ulrich (1939-)
Resident Minister of the Manitoba Buddhist Temple in Canada

Maia Daguerre

Water flows over these hands.
May I use them skillfully
to preserve our precious planet.

Thich Nhat Hanh (1926-)
Vietnamese Zen Buddhist Monk, Teacher, Author, Poet and Peace Activist

From the book "Present Moment Wonderful Moment: Mindfulness Verses for Daily Living"

The garden is rich with diversity,
With plants of a hundred families,
In the space between the trees,
With all the colors and fragrances.

Basil, mint and lavender,
Great Mystery,
Keep my remembrance pure,
Raspberry, apple, rose,
Great Mystery,
Fill my heart with love,
Dill, anise, tansy,
Holy winds blow in me.

Rhododendron, zinnia,
May my prayer be beautiful.

May my remembrance,
O Great Mystery,
Be as incense to thee,
In the sacred grove of eternity,
As I smell and remember
The ancient forests of earth.

Traditional Chinook Prayer
Native American Indigenous People

Maia Daguerre

Through the Silence of Nature

Through the silence of nature I attain thy divine peace.

O sublime nature, in thy stillness let my heart rest.

Thou art patiently awaiting the moment to manifest through the silence of sublime nature.

O nature sublime, speak to me through silence, for I am awaiting in silence like you the call of God.

O nature sublime, through thy silence I hear thy cry.

My heart is tuned to the quietness that the stillness of nature inspires.

Inayat Khan (1882 – 1927)
Indian Musician, Mystic Philosopher and Founder of The Sufi Movement

O our Mother the Earth,
O our Father the Sky,
Your children are we,
And with tired backs
We bring you the gifts that you love.

Then weave for us a garment of brightness.

May the warp be the bright light of morning;
May the fringes be the falling rain;
May the borders be the standing rainbow.

Thus weave for us a garment of brightness,
That we may walk fittingly where birds sing;
That we may walk fittingly where grass is green.

O our Mother the Earth,
O our Father the Sky.

Tewa Song
Native American Indigenous People

Maia Daguerre

Four Elements Medicine Wheel

O Great Spirit of the North,
Invisible Spirit of the Air,
And of the fresh, cool winds,
O vast and boundless Grandfather Sky,
Your living breath animates all life.
Yours is the power of clarity and strength,
Power to hear the inner sounds,
To sweep out the old patterns,
And to bring change and challenge,
The ecstasy of movement and the dance.
We pray that we may be aligned with you,
So that your power may flow through us,
And be expressed by us,
For the good of this planet,
And all living beings upon it.

O Great Spirit of the West,
Spirit of the Great Waters,
Of rain, rivers, lakes and springs,
O Grandmother Ocean
Deep matrix, womb of all life.
Power to dissolve boundaries,
To release holdings,
Power to taste and to feel,
To cleanse and to heal,
Great blissful darkness of peace.
We pray that we may be aligned with you,
So that your powers may flow through us,
And be expressed by us,
For the good of this planet,
And all living beings upon it.

O Great Spirit of the East,
Radiance of the rising Sun,
Spirit of new beginnings,
O Grandfather Fire,

Mother Earth

Great nuclear fire of the Sun.
Power of life-energy, vital spark,
Power to see far, and to imagine with boldness.
Power to purify our senses,
Our hearts and our minds.
We pray that we may be aligned with you,
So that your powers may flow through us,
And be expressed by us,
For the good of this planet Earth,
And all living beings upon it.

O Great Spirit of the South,
Protector of the fruitful land,
And of all green and growing things,
The noble trees and grasses,
Grandmother Earth, Soul of Nature.
Great power of the receptive,
Of nurturance and endurance,
Power to grow and bring forth
Flowers of the field, fruits of the garden.
We pray that we may be aligned with you,
So that your powers may flow through us,
And be expressed by us,
For the good of this planet Earth,
And all living beings upon it.

Ralph Metzner (1936-)
German psychologist, writer and researcher involved in the study of "Altered States of Consciousness". Worked with Timothy Leary and Richard Alpert on the Harvard Psilocybin Projects.

From the book "Allies for Awakening - Guidelines for productive and safe experiences with entheogens"

Maia Daguerre

HaShem:

Grant me the ability to be alone!

May it be my custom to go outdoors each day among the trees and grass —among all growing things, and there may I be alone, and enter into prayer, to talk with the One to whom I belong.

May I express there everything in my heart, and may all the foliage of the field – all grasses, trees and plants —awake at my coming, to send the powers of their life into the words of my prayer, so that my prayer and speech are made whole through the life and the spirit of all growing things, which are made as one by their transcendent Source.

May I then pour out the words of my heart before your Presence like water, *HaShem*, and lift up my hands to You in song, on my behalf, and that of my children!

Rabbi Nachman ben Feiga of Breslov (1772-1810)
Grandson of the famous Rabbi Baal Shem Tov and member of the Hasidic movement that combined the esoteric secrets of Judaism ("The Kabbalah") with in-depth Torah scholarship

"*HaShem*" *(lit. "The name") is used to refer to God, when avoiding God's more formal title, "Adonai" (lit. "My Master")*

Hymn XXX - To Earth the mother of all

I will sing of well-founded Earth, mother of all, eldest of all beings. She feeds all creatures that are in the world, all that go upon the goodly land, and all that are in the paths of the seas, and all that fly: all these are fed of her store. Through you, O queen, men are blessed in their children and blessed in their harvests, and to you it belongs to give means of life to mortal men and to take it away. Happy is the man whom you delight to honour! He has all things abundantly: his fruitful land is laden with corn, his pastures are covered with cattle, and his house is filled with good things. Such men rule orderly in their cities of fair women: great riches and wealth follow them: their sons exult with ever-fresh delight, and their daughters in flower-laden bands play and skip merrily over the soft flowers of the field. Thus is it with those whom you honour O holy goddess, bountiful spirit.

Hail, Mother of the gods, wife of starry Heaven; freely bestow upon me for this my song substance that cheers the heart! And now I will remember you and another song also.

From "The Homeric Hymns" (8th / 6th century BCE)
Anonymous Ancient Greek Hymns

Translated by Hugh G. Evelyn-White (1914)

Maia Daguerre

But ask the animals, now, and they shall teach you;
   the birds of the sky, and they shall tell you.

Or speak to the earth, and it shall teach you.
   The fish of the sea shall declare to you.

The Book of Job 12:7-8 (6th century BCE)

Chapter VII

ABUNDANCE

Maia Daguerre

Prayer for Sustenance

My help is from the Lord, who made heaven and earth. Cast thy burden upon the Lord, and he shall sustain thee. Mark the perfect man, and behold the upright; for the latter end of that man is peace. Trust in the Lord, and do good; dwell in the land, and feed upon faithfulness. Behold, God is my salvation; I will trust and will not be afraid: for Jah the Lord is my strength and song, and he is become my salvation.

O Sovereign of the universe, in thy holy words it is written, saying, He that trusteth in the Lord, lovingkindness shall compass him, about; and it is written, And thou givest life to them all. O Lord God of truth, vouchsafe blessing and prosperity upon all the work of my hands, for I trust in thee that thou wilt so bless me through my occupation and calling, that I may be enabled to support myself and the members of my household with ease and not with pain, by lawful and not by forbidden means, unto life and peace. In me also let the scripture be fulfilled, Cast thy burden upon the Lord, and he shall sustain thee. Amen!

Traditional Jewish Prayer
From "The Standard Prayer Book" translated by Simeon Singer (1915)

Hoshbam (Prayer at Dawn)

I pray with benedictions for a benefit, and for the good, even for the entire creation of the holy and the clean;

I beseech for them for the generation which is now alive, for that which is just coming into life, and for that which shall be hereafter.

And I pray for that sanctity which leads to prosperity, and which has long afforded shelter, which goes on hand in hand with it, which joins it in its walk, and of itself becoming its close companion as it delivers forth its precepts, bearing every form of healing virtue which comes to us in waters, appertains to cattle, or is found in plants, and overwhelming all the harmful malice of the Daêvas, and their servants, who might harm this dwelling and its lord, bringing good gifts, and better blessings, given very early, and later gifts, leading to successes, and for a long time giving shelter.

And so the greatest, and the best, and most beautiful benefits of sanctity fall likewise to our lot for the sacrifice, homage, propitiation, and the praise of the Bountiful Immortals, for the bringing prosperity to this abode, and for the prosperity of the entire creation of the holy, and the clean, and as for this, so for the opposition of the entire evil creation.

And I pray for this as I praise through Righteousness, I who am beneficent, chose who are likewise of a better mind.

Zoroastrian Prayer (2nd millennium BCE)

Excerpt from the "Khorda Avesta", collections of Zoroastrian religious texts Zoroastrianism is one of the world's oldest religions that arose in the eastern region of the ancient Persian Empire and influenced other later religions including Judaism, Gnosticism, Christianity and Islam

Maia Daguerre

O God, when I have food,

help me to remember the hungry;

When I have work, help me to remember the jobless;

When I have a home, help me to remember those who have no home at all;

When I am without pain, help me to remember those who suffer;

And remembering, help me to destroy my complacency, bestir my compassion, and be concerned enough to help, by word and deed, those who cry out for what we take for granted.

Amen.

Samuel F. Pugh (1850–1922)
United States Representative from Kentucky

Pir

Inspirer of my mind,
Consoler of my heart,
Healer of my spirit,
Thy presence lifteth me from earth to heaven;
Thy words flow as the sacred river;
Thy thought riseth as a divine spring;
Thy tender feelings waken sympathy in my heart.
Beloved Teacher,
Thy very being is forgiveness.
The clouds of doubt and fear are scattered
By thy piercing glance;
All ignorance vanishes
In thy illuminating presence;
A new hope is born in my heart
By breathing thy peaceful atmosphere.
O inspiring Guide
Through life's puzzling ways,
In thee I feel abundance of blessing.

Inayat Khan (1882 – 1927)
Indian Musician, Mystic Philosopher and Founder of The Sufi Movement

"*Pir*" *means "old person," "elder," in Persian language. It is a title for a spiritual guide. In Sufism, a Pir's role is to guide and instruct his disciples on the Sufi path.*

Maia Daguerre

Ode 279

Abundant is the year,

With much millet and much rice;

And we have our high granaries,

With myriads, and hundreds of thousands, and millions of measures in them;

For spirits and sweet spirits,

To present our ancestors, male and female,

And to supply all our ceremonies.

The blessings sent down on us are of every kind.

Traditional Chinese Poem

From the "Shi Jing: The Book of Songs" (11th / 8th century BCE), the oldest existing collection of Chinese poetry. It has a major place in the canonical works associated with Confucianism.
Translated by James Legge (1899)

He is the One who sent down water from the sky

for you, from it you drink, and from it emerge the trees that you wander around in.

He brings forth with it vegetation and olives and palm trees and grapes and from all the fruits. In that are signs for a people who think.

And He committed for you the night and the day, and the sun and the moon, and the stars are committed by His command. In that are signs for a people who comprehend.

And what He has placed for you on Earth in various colors. In that are signs for a people who remember.

And He is the One who committed the sea, that you may eat from it a tender meat, and that you may extract from it pearls that you wear. And you see the ships flowing through it, so that you may seek from His bounty, and that you may be thankful.

And He has cast into the Earth stabilizers so that it does not sway with you, and rivers, and paths, perhaps you will be guided.

And landmarks, and by the stars they use to guide.

Is the One who creates the same as one who does not create? Will you not remember?

And if you count the blessings of God you will not be able to fathom them. God is Forgiving, Merciful.

Qur'an 16:10-18 (7th century CE)

Maia Daguerre

Psalm 35:27

Let them shout for joy and be glad, who favor my righteous cause.

Yes, let them say continually, "Yahweh be magnified,
   who has pleasure in the prosperity of his servant!"

Attributed to King David (10th century BCE)
From "The Book of Psalms"

Prayer of The Sower

Blessing to the seed I scatter,
Where it falls upon the meadow
By the grace of *Ukko* mighty,
Through the open finger spaces
Of the hand that all things fashioned.

Queen of meadow-land and pasture!

Bid the earth unlock her treasures.

Bid the soil the young seed nourish.

Never shall their teeming forces,
Never shall their strength prolific
Fail to nourish and sustain us,
If the Daughters of Creation,
They, the free and bounteous givers,
Still extend their gracious favor
Offer still their strong protection.

Rise, O Earth!

From out thy slumbers
Bid the soil unlock her treasures!

Ancient Finnish Pagan Prayer

From "Pagan Prayers" by Marah Ellis Ryan (1913)
"Ukko" means "male grandparent," "old man," and is the god of the sky, weather, harvest and thunder in Finnish mythology.

Maia Daguerre

It's Harvest Time

It's harvest time,
It's harvest time,
How rich is nature's yield
In fruit of earth
And bush and tree,
From orchard, farm and field.
It's autumn time,
It's autumn time,
When leaves turn gold and red.
In smiling sky
And land and sea
God's glories are outspread.
It's *Sukkos* time,
It's *Sukkos* time,
This day of our Thanksgiving.
We hymn the praise of God above for all the joys of living.

Traditional Israeli Song

"Sukkos" is a biblical Jewish holiday. During this time, meals are eaten inside the "sukkah" (temporary hut) and many people sleep there as well, recalling the ancient costume of the agricultural workers to live in temporary dwelling during harvesting.

Every time I feel the spirit

Movin' in my heart
I will pray.
Every time I feel the spirit
Movin' in my heart
I will pray.
Up on the mountains
My Lord spoke;
Out of His mouth
Came fire and smoke;
An' all around me
Looked so shine,
I asked my Lord
If all was mine.

African-American spiritual dating to before the US Civil War

The Radical Empowerment PowerShift Process

1. Spiritual Intelligence

I recognize that there is only one power in the Universe and that, through the gift of Spiritual Intelligence, I am able to connect with and utilize this Divine power for good purpose in my life. I am one with Universal Intelligence and It expresses itself through me.

2. Radical Forgiveness

In recognition of my Oneness with Universal Intelligence, I am willing to let go of any and all forms of victim consciousness and to 'radically' forgive anyone and anything over which I might still feel any form of grievance or discomfort. I am willing to see and feel the Divine perfection in all situations.

3. Surrender

I believe that the Universe is a place of Divine Abundance and that, by opening myself in humility and with an egoless mind to the power of Universal Intelligence, I can co-create my life. Even as I ask for what I want, I am open to receive the abundance of the Universe in whatever form it arrives knowing that I will always be divinely blessed.

4. Radical Manifestation

As I connect now with my own Divinely gifted, creative power to manifest form and create circumstances in this world, I am aware that the power comes only from Source — Universal Intelligence. In knowing this, I make my request to Source for guidance and help in manifesting _____.

5. Radical Empowerment — Group Response

"_____, we love and support you in your power and know that the connection you have made with the most powerful creative force in the Universe is empowering you now to manifest all that you desire — and we know that it is already done."

6. Gratitude

Thank you. Knowing that time and space is not operative here and that it is indeed already done, I am allowing myself to feel the emotions of already having my requests granted and the guidance given me. I am feeling _____.

Colin Tipping (1941-)
English author of "Radical Forgiveness: Making Room for the Miracle" and the Tipping Method

Best performed with a group, this prayer is said to increase abundance vibrations. Its purpose is to help each other manifest what they want and achieve their goals by tapping into and leveraging the group's spiritual intelligence.

Maia Daguerre

Lord Jesus Christ, you are the sun
that always rises but never sets.

You are the source of all life, creating and sustaining every living thing.

You are the source of all food, material and spiritual, nourishing us in both body and soul.

You are the light that dispels the clouds of error and doubt, and goes before me every hour of the day, guiding my thoughts and actions.

May I walk in your light, be sustained by your mercy, and be warmed by your love.

Amen.

Erasmus of Rotterdam (1466–1536)
Dutch Renaissance Humanist and Catholic Priest

Prayer to Lord *Ganesh*

Lord Ganesh
who wears a white garment,
who is all-pervading,
who has a bright complexion,
who has four arms,
who has an ever smiling face,
upon that God,
I meditate for removal
of all obstacles.

Traditional Hindu Prayer

"Ganesh," the remover of obstacles, is one of the best-known and most worshipped deities in the Hindu pantheon.

Maia Daguerre

Blessed are we
who can laugh at ourselves,
for we shall never cease to be amused.

Unknown Author

Chapter VIII

GRATITUDE

Maia Daguerre

We give thanks for all those who are moved,
in their lives, to heal and protect the earth,
in small ways and in large.

Blessings on the composters, the gardeners, the breeders of worms and mushrooms,
the soil-builders, those who cleanse the waters and purify the air,
all those who clean up the messes others have made.

Blessings on those who defend trees and who plant trees,
who guard the forests and who renew the forests.

Blessings on those who learn to heal the grasslands and renew the streams,
on those who prevent erosion, who restore the salmon and the fisheries,
who guard the healing herbs and who know the lore of the wild plants.

Blessings on those who heal the cities and bring them alive again with excitement and creativity and love.

Gratitude and blessings to all who stand against greed, who risk themselves,
to those who have bled and been wounded, and to those who have given their lives in service of the earth.

May all the healers of the earth find their own healing.

May they be fueled by passionate love for the earth.

May they know their fear but not be stopped by fear.

May they feel their anger and yet not be ruled by rage.

May they honor their grief but not be paralyzed by sorrow.

May they transform fear, rage, and grief into compassion and the inspiration to act in service of what they love.

May they find the help, the resources, the courage, the luck, the strength, the love,
the health, the joy that they need to do the work.

May they be in the right place, at the right time, in the right way.

May they bring alive a great awakening, open a listening ear to hear the earth's voice,
transform imbalance to balance, hate and greed to love.

Blessed be the healers of the earth.

Starhawk (1951-)
American writer and activist.

Excerpt from "The Earth Path: Grounding Your Spirit in the Rhythms of Nature"

Maia Daguerre

The sun brings forth the beginning.
The moon holds it in darkness.
As above, so below.
For there is no greater magic in all the world
Than that of people joined together in love.

Wiccan Blessing

Also termed "Pagan Witchcraft," Wicca is a contemporary religious movement, developed in England during the first half of the 20th century, that draws upon a diverse set of ancient pagan and hermetic motifs for its theological structure and ritual practice.

Invocation to Ormazd

In the name of God, the giver, forgiver, rich in love, praise be to the name of *Ormazd*, the God with the name who always was, always is, and always will be; the heavenly among the heavenly, with the name: "From whom alone is derived rule."

With all strength bring I thanks.

All good do I accept at thy command O God, and think, and speak, and do it.

I believe in the pure law; by every good work seek I forgiveness for all sins.

I keep pure the six powers: thought, speech, work, memory, mind and understanding.

According to thy will am I able to accomplish.

O accomplisher of good, thy honor, with good thoughts, good works.

I enter on the shining way to Paradise; may the fearful terror of hell not overcome me!

May I step over the bridge *Chinevat*.

May I attain Paradise with much perfume, and all brightness.

Praise be to the Overseer, the Lord, who rewards those who accomplish good deeds according to his own wish, and at last purifies even the wicked ones of hell.

Zoroastrian Prayer (2nd millennium BCE)
From the book "Pagan Rituals, Liturgies and Prayers" by Marah Ellis Ryan (1913)

Zoroastrianism is one of the world's oldest religions that arose in the eastern region of the ancient Persian Empire and influenced other later religions including Judaism, Gnosticism, Christianity and Islam.

"Ormazd" is the name for the creator and sole god of Zoroastrianism.
"Bridge Chinevat" is the sifting bridge that separates the world of the living from the world of the dead.

Maia Daguerre

Thanksgiving Day Prayer

O God, we thank you for this earth, our home, for the wide sky and the blessed sun, for the salt sea and the running water, for the everlasting hills and the never-resting winds, for trees and the common grass underfoot.

We thank you for our senses, by which we hear the songs of birds, and see the splendor of the summer fields, and taste of the autumn fruits, and rejoice in the feel of the snow, and smell the breath of the spring.

Grant us a heart wide open to all this beauty;

And save our souls from being so blind that we pass unseeing when even the common thornbush is aflame with your glory,

O God our creator, who lives and reigns forever and ever.

Walter Rauschenbusch (1861–1918)
Christian Theologian and Baptist Pastor

Lord we Praise You for cities and towns,

factories and farms, flowers and trees, sea and sky.

Lord we praise You for the world and its beauty.

For family and friends, neighbors and cousins.

Lord, we thank You for friendship and love.

For kind hearts, smiling faces, and helping hands.

Lord, we praise You for those who care for others.

For commandments that teach us how to live.

Lord we thank You for those who help us to understand your laws.

And for making us one family on earth, the children of One God.

Lord we praise You, who made all people different, yet alike.

Jewish Liturgy

Maia Daguerre

Ohen:ton Karihwatehkwen ("The Words that Come Before All Else")

Today we have gathered and we see that the cycles of life continue.

We have been given the duty to live in balance and harmony with each other and all living things. So now, we bring our minds together as one as we give greetings and thanks to each other as people.

Now our minds are one.

We are all thankful to our Mother, the Earth, for she gives us all that we need for life. She supports our feet as we walk about upon her. It gives us joy that she continues to care for us as she has from the beginning of time. To our mother, we send greetings and thanks.

Now our minds are one.

We give thanks to all the waters of the world for quenching our thirst and providing us with strength. Water is life. We know its power in many forms - waterfalls and rain, mists and streams, rivers and oceans. With one mind, we send greetings and thanks to the spirit of Water.

Now our minds are one.

We turn our minds to the all the Fish life in the water. They were instructed to cleanse and purify the water. They also give themselves to us as food. We are grateful that we can still find pure water. So, we turn now to the Fish and send our greetings and thanks.

Now our minds are one.

Now we turn toward the vast fields of Plant life. As far as the eye can see, the Plants grow, working many wonders. They sustain many life forms. With our minds gathered together, we give thanks and look forward to seeing Plant life for many generations to come.

Now our minds are one.

With one mind, we turn to honor and thank all the Food Plants we harvest from the garden. Since the beginning of time, the grains, vegetables, beans and berries have helped the people survive. Many other living things draw strength from them too. We gather all the Plant Foods together as one and send them a greeting of thanks.

Now our minds are one.

Now we turn to all the Medicine herbs of the world. From the beginning they were instructed to take away sickness. They are always waiting and ready to heal us. We are happy there are still among us those special few who remember how to use these plants for healing. With one mind, we send greetings and thanks to the Medicines and to the keepers of the Medicines.

Now our minds are one.

We gather our minds together to send greetings and thanks to all the Animal life in the world. They have many things to teach us as people. We are honored by them when they give up their lives so we may use their bodies as food for our people. We see them near our homes and in the deep forests. We are glad they are still here and we hope that it will always be so.

Now our minds are one.

We now turn our thoughts to the Trees. The Earth has many families of Trees who have their own instructions and uses. Some provide us with shelter and shade, others with fruit, beauty and other useful things. Many people of the world use a Tree as a symbol of peace and strength. With one mind, we greet and thank the Tree life.

Now our minds are one.

We put our minds together as one and thank all the Birds who move and fly about over our heads. The Creator gave them beautiful songs. Each day they remind us to enjoy and appreciate life. The Eagle was chosen to be their leader. To all the Birds -

from the smallest to the largest - we send our joyful greetings and thanks.

Now our minds are one.

We are all thankful to the powers we know as the Four Winds. We hear their voices in the moving air as they refresh us and purify the air we breathe. They help us to bring the change of seasons. From the four directions they come, bringing us messages and giving us strength. With one mind, we send our greetings and thanks to the Four Winds.

Now our minds are one.

Now we turn to the west where our grandfathers, the Thunder Beings, live. With lightning and thundering voices, they bring with them the water that renews life. We are thankful that they keep those evil things made by Okwiseres underground. We bring our minds together as one to send greetings and thanks to our Grandfathers, the Thunderers.

Now our minds are one.

We now send greetings and thanks to our eldest Brother, the Sun. Each day without fail he travels the sky from east to west, bringing the light of a new day. He is the source of all the fires of life. With one mind, we send greetings and thanks to our Brother, the Sun. Now our minds are one.

We put our minds together to give thanks to our oldest Grandmother, the Moon, who lights the night-time sky. She is the leader of woman all over the world, and she governs the movement of the ocean tides. By her changing face we measure time, and it is the Moon who watches over the arrival of children here on Earth. With one mind, we send greetings and thanks to our Grandmother, the Moon.

Now our minds are one.

We give thanks to the Stars who are spread across the sky like jewelry. We see them in the night, helping the Moon to light the darkness and bringing dew to the gardens and growing things. When we travel at night, they guide us home. With our minds

Gratitude

gathered together as one, we send greetings and thanks to the Stars.

Now our minds are one.

We gather our minds to greet and thank the enlightened Teachers who have come to help throughout the ages. When we forget how to live in harmony, they remind us of the way we were instructed to live as people. With one mind, we send greetings and thanks to these caring teachers.

Now our minds are one.

Now we turn our thoughts to the creator, or Great Spirit, and send greetings and thanks for all the gifts of Creation. Everything we need to live a good life is here on this Mother Earth. For all the love that is still around us, we gather our minds together as one and send our choicest words of greetings and thanks to the Creator.

Now our minds are one.

We have now arrived at the place where we end our words. Of all the things we have named, it was not our intention to leave anything out. If something was forgotten, we leave it to each individual to send such greetings and thanks in their own way.

Now our minds are one.

Haudenosaunee version of the Thanksgiving Address

Central prayer for the "Haudenosaunee", also known as the Iroquois Confederacy or Six Native American Nations — Mohawk, Oneida, Cayuga, Onondaga, Seneca, and Tuscarora.

The Haudenosaunee open and close every social and religious meeting with the Thanksgiving Address. It is also said as a daily sunrise prayer, and is an ancient message of peace and appreciation of Mother Earth and her inhabitants. It reflects their relationship of giving thanks for life and the world around them. When one recites the Thanksgiving Address, the Natural World is thanked, and in thanking each life-sustaining force, one becomes spiritually tied to each of the forces of the Natural and Spiritual World.

Maia Daguerre

The Blessing of Unanswered Prayers

I asked for strength that I might achieve;
I was made weak that I might learn humbly to obey.

I asked for health that I might do greater things;
I was given infirmity that I might do better things.

I asked for riches that I might be happy;
I was given poverty that I might be wise.

I asked for power that I might have the praise of men;
I was given weakness that I might feel the need of God.

I asked for all things that I might enjoy life;
I was given life that I might enjoy all things.

I got nothing that I had asked for;
But everything that I had hoped for.

Almost despite myself my unspoken prayers were answered;
I am, among all men, most richly blessed.

Unknown Author

Great and Eternal Mystery of Life,

creator of all things, I give thanks for the beauty You put in every single one of Your creations.

I am grateful that you did not fail in making every stone, plant, creature and human being, a perfect and whole part of the Sacred Hoop.

I am grateful that you have allowed me to see the strength and beauty of all my relations.

My humble request is that all of the Children of Earth will learn to see the same perfection in themselves.

May none of your human children doubt or question your wisdom, grace and sense of wholeness in giving all of Creation a right to be living extensions of your perfect love.

Unknown Native American Prayer

Maia Daguerre

If the only prayer you said
was thank you,
that would be enough.

Meister Eckhart (1260–1328)
German theologian, Philosopher and Mystic

Gratitude

Let us be grateful to people who make us happy;

They are the charming gardeners
who make our souls blossom.

Marcel Proust (1871–1922)
French Novelist, Critic and Essayist

Maia Daguerre

We return thanks to our mother, the earth,
which sustains us.
We return thanks to the rivers and streams,
which supply us with waters.
We return thanks to all herbs,
which furnish medicine for the cure of our diseases.
We return thanks to the corn, and to her sisters,
the beans and the squashes, which give us life.
We return thanks to the wind,
which moving the air has banished diseases.
We return thanks to the moon and the stars,
which have given us their light when the sun was gone.
We return thanks to the sun,
that he has looked upon the earth with a beneficent eye.
Lastly, we return thanks to the Great Spirit,
in whom is embodied all goodness, and who directs all things for the good of his children.

Iroquois Prayer

Confederacy of Six Native American Nations — Mohawk, Oneida, Cayuga, Onondaga, Seneca and Tuscarora

O My Father, Great Elder,
I have no words to thank you,
But with your deep wisdom
I am sure that you can see
How I value your glorious gifts.

O My Father, when I look upon your greatness,
I am confounded with awe.

O Great Elder,
Ruler of all things earthly and heavenly,
I am your warrior,
Ready to act in accordance with your will.

Traditional Prayer of the Kikuyu People

The Kikuyu are the largest ethnic group in Kenya, Africa.

Chapter IX

HEALING

First Epistle to the Corinthians - Chapter 13

If I speak with the languages of men and of angels, but don't have love, I have become sounding brass, or a clanging cymbal.

If I have the gift of prophecy, and know all mysteries and all knowledge; and if I have all faith, so as to remove mountains, but don't have love, I am nothing.

If I dole out all my goods to feed the poor, and if I give my body to be burned, but don't have love, it profits me nothing.

Love is patient and is kind; love doesn't envy.

Love doesn't brag, is not proud, doesn't behave itself inappropriately, doesn't seek its own way, is not provoked, takes no account of evil; doesn't rejoice in unrighteousness, but rejoices with the truth; bears all things, believes all things, hopes all things, endures all things.

Love never fails.

But where there are prophecies, they will be done away with.

Where there are various languages, they will cease.

Where there is knowledge, it will be done away with.

For we know in part, and we prophesy in part; but when that which is complete has come, then that which is partial will be done away with.

When I was a child, I spoke as a child, I felt as a child, I thought as a child.

Now that I have become a man, I have put away childish things.

For now we see in a mirror, dimly, but then face to face.

Now I know in part, but then I will know fully, even as I was also fully known.

But now faith, hope, and love remain—these three.

The greatest of these is love.

Attributed to Saint Paul (5-67 CE)

Maia Daguerre

Nayaz

Beloved Lord, Almighty God!
Through the rays of the sun
Through the waves of the air
Through the All-pervading Life in space
Purify and revivify me
And I pray:
Heal my body, heart, and soul.
Amen.

Inayat Khan (1882–1927)
Indian Musician, Mystic Philosopher and Founder of The Sufi Movement

Prayer to the World

Let the rain come and wash away the ancient grudges, the bitter hatreds, held and nurtured over generations.

Let the rain wash away the memory of the hurt, the neglect.

Then let the sun come out and fill the sky with rainbows.

Let the warmth of the sun heal us wherever we are broken.

Let it burn away the fog so that we can see each other clearly.

So that we can see beyond labels, beyond accents, gender or skin color.

Let the warmth and brightness of the sun melt our selfishness, so that we can share the joys, and feel the sorrows of our neighbors.

And let the light of the sun be so strong that we will see all people as our neighbors.

Let the earth, nourished by rain, bring forth flowers to surround us with beauty.

And let the mountains teach our hearts to reach upward to heaven.

Amen.

Rabbi Harold Kushner (1935-)
American Rabbi and Author

Maia Daguerre

O Allah! I am your servant,
Son of Your male servant,
And son of Your female servant;

My forehead is in Your Hand,
Your judgment is exact,
Your decision about me is just.

I ask You by every name of Yours
Which You have called Yourself,
Or revealed in a Book of Yours,
Or taught to any of Your servants,
Or reserved within Your unrevealed Knowledge,
To make the Qur'an
A spring to my heart,
A light in my chest,
That it removes my sadness,
And erase my anguish.

Traditional Islamic Prayer attributed to Prophet Muhammad (570-632)

Invocation

O Love of God,
Descend into my heart;
Enlighten the dark corners of this neglected dwelling,
And scatter there your cheerful beams.

Dwell in the soul
That longs to be Your temple;
Water that barren soil
Overrun with weeds and briars
And lost for lack of cultivating.

Make it fruitful with Your dew.

Come, dear refreshment of those who languish;
Come, Star and Guide of those who sail amidst tempests.

You are the haven of the tossed and shipwrecked.

Come now, Glory and Crown of the living,
As well as the safeguard of the dying.

Come, Sacred Spirit;
Come, and fit me
To receive You.

Saint Augustine (354-430)
Early Christian theologian and philosopher whose writings influenced the development of Western Christianity and Western philosophy

Heavenly Father,
Charge my body
With Thy vitality.
Charge my mind
With Thy spiritual power.
Charge my soul
With Thy joy,
Thine immortality.

O Father, Thine unlimited
And all-healing power is in me.
Manifest Thy light
Through the darkness
Of my ignorance.

O Eternal Energy,
Awaken in me conscious will,
Conscious vitality,
Conscious health,
Conscious realization.

Paramahansa Yogananda (1893–1952)
Indian Yogi and Guru who introduced millions of westerners to the teachings of meditation

From "Metaphysical Meditations"

Exorcism of Spirits of Disease

The noxious god, the noxious spirit of the neck, the neck-spirit of the desert, the neck-spirit of the mountains, the neck-spirit of the sea, the neck-spirit of the morass, the noxious spirit of the city, this noxious wind which seizes the body and the health of the body.

Spirit of Heaven, remember! Spirit of Earth, remember!

He who makes an image which injures the man, an evil face, an evil eye, an evil mouth, an evil tongue, evil lips, an evil poison.

Spirit of Heaven, remember! Spirit of Earth, remember!

The cruel spirit, the strong spirit of the head, the head-spirit that departs not, the head-spirit that goes not forth, the head-spirit that will not go, the noxious head spirit.

Spirit of Heaven, remember! Spirit of Earth, remember!

May *Nin-cigal*, the wife of *Nin-a'su*, turn her face toward another place; may the noxious spirit go forth and seize another. May the propitious spirit and the propitious *genii* settle upon his body.

Spirit of Heaven, remember! Spirit of Earth, remember!

May *Nebs*, the great steward, the recliner supreme among the gods, like the god who has begotten him, seize upon his head; against his life may he not break forth.

Spirit of Heaven, remember! Spirit of Earth, remember!

On the sick man by the sacrifice of mercy may perfect health shine like bronze; may the Sun-god give this man life; may *Merodach*, the eldest son of the deep, give him strength, prosperity and health.

Spirit of Heaven, remember! Spirit of Earth, remember!

Ancient Babylonian Prayer For Health
From "Pagan Prayers" by Marah Ellis Ryan (1913)

"Nin-cigal" is the Goddess of the House of Death.
"Genii" are supernatural creatures.
"Merodach" is the chief of the Babylonian deities.

Maia Daguerre

When the wind blows
– That is my medicine.

When it rains
– That is my medicine.

When it hails
– That is my medicine.

When it becomes clear after a storm
– That is my medicine.

Unknown Author

Violet Flame Decrees - Healing

"I AM" the Mighty Presence of this Alert Radiant Energy surging through my mind and body, dismissing everything unlike Itself.

I take my stand in this Alert, Radiant Energy and Joy for all time.

"I AM" the Presence charging this body with pure electronic Energy.

"I AM" the Perfect Activity of every organ and cell of my body.

Perfect Health now manifest in every organ of my body.

The Perfect Intelligent Activity in this body.

The All-Christ Healing by the "Mighty I AM".
The All-Christ Healing by God's Own Hand.
The All-Christ Healing by God's Love Ray.

The All-Christ Healing
"I AM" today.
The All-Christ Healing
"I AM" to stay.
The All-Christ Healing
"I AM" God's Way.
The All-Christ Healing
"I AM" by God's Precipitating Ray.
The All-Christ Healing.
The Miracle Way.
The All-Christ Healing
Forever holds sway.

"Mighty I AM Presence", come forth through my mind and body.

Produce Perfection and hold Dominion here forever.

Violet Flame Healing Now.

The Law of Instantaneous healing.

The Perfect Activity of every organ and cell of my body.

The Perfect, Intelligent Activity of this body.

The "Presence" charging this body with Pure Electronic energy.

"I AM" my Perfect Sight.
"I AM" my Perfect Hearing.
"I AM" my Perfect Action of the throat.

"Mighty I AM Presence," charge my aura with instantaneous healing to everybody that comes into my presence, and set all free in the Service of the Light.

The "Mighty I AM Presence" is the only Healing Presence, and through it, I have the right to command all outer activity to be silent and obey my command.

"Mighty I AM presence," great host of Ascended Masters, Mighty Legions of Light, great Angelic Host, Mighty Cosmic Beings, and the great beings from the Healing Temple of Light.

Come forth in Your Mightiest Combined Healing Power.

We call on the Law of Forgiveness for ourselves and all mankind, and we forgive all mistakes of all mankind forever.

Blaze forth through every human body on Earth the most Instantaneous Activity and Purifying Power of the Violet Consuming Flame.

Annihilate the cause and effect of all disease from humanity forever.

Produce Ascended Master Healings and Perfection for all and hold Your Dominion forever!

We thank Thee Thou dost always answer our every Call, and it is eternally sustained and ever-expanding.

"Mighty I AM Presence," these are Your hands.

Pour forth through them always Thy Healing Miracles and Full Perfection.

"Mighty I AM Presence," charge my aura with instantaneous healing to everybody that comes into my presence, and set all free in the Service of the Light.

"I AM!" The Resurrection, the Life, the Health, and the Light of my body, made manifest in and through my flesh today.

Saint Germain Foundation

The violet flame is a unique spiritual energy that has the highest frequency in the visible spectrum of the light. Saints and adepts throughout the ages have known how to use the violet flame, but it was only released to the public earlier this century by an Ascended Master called Saint Germain. The violet flame works by changing "vibrations", transmuting negative energy. It is said that it does not simply surround and remove the energy, but transforms it into light.

The "I AM" Presence is a sphere of light known to Hindus as Brahma, to Buddhists as the Dharmakaya and to Christians as God the Father. It is the spirit of God individualized for each soul. The "I AM" Presence is surrounded by seven concentric spheres of cosmic consciousness called causal body.

An Ascended Master is a Being of Light who is not in body. They have paid all their karma, left the cycle of rebirth and attained mastery over themselves.

Maia Daguerre

The Guest House

This being human is a guest house.
Every morning a new arrival.

A joy, a depression, a meanness,
Some momentary awareness comes
As an unexpected visitor.

Welcome and entertain them all!

Even if they are a crowd of sorrows,
Who violently sweep your house
Empty of its furniture,
Still, treat each guest honorably.

He may be clearing you out
For some new delight.

The dark thought, the shame, the malice,
Meet them at the door laughing and invite them in.

Be grateful for whatever comes,
Because each has been sent
As a guide from beyond.

Rumi (1207–1273)
Sufi Poet and Mystic

Translated by Coleman Barks

And I saw the river
Over which every soul must pass
To reach the kingdom of heaven
And the name of that river
Was suffering.

And I saw the boat
Which carries souls across the river
And the name of that boat
Was love.

Saint John of the Cross (1542-1591)
Spanish Mystic and Roman Catholic Saint

Maia Daguerre

I cleanse myself of all selfishness,
resentment,
critical feelings for my fellow beings,
self-condemnation
and misinterpretation of my life experiences.

I bathe myself in generosity,
appreciation,
praise and gratitude for my fellow beings,
self-acceptance
and enlightened understanding of my life experiences.

Unknown Author

Healing

The great sea moves me, sets me adrift.

It moves me like algae on stones
in running brook water.

The vault of heaven moves me.
Mighty weather storms through my soul.

It carries me with it.
Trembling with joy.

Uvavnuk (20^b century CE)
Female Shamaness and Oral Poet of the Inuit People

Inuit are indigenous peoples inhabiting the Arctic regions of Greenland, Canada, and Alaska

Maia Daguerre

Hymn to The Unknown God

O Ruler!

Lord of the universe,
Whether thou art male,
Whether thou art female,
Lord of reproduction,
Wherever thou mayest be!

O Lord of divination!

Where art thou?

Thou mayest be above,
Thou mayest be below,
Or perhaps around
Thy splendid throne and sceptre.

O hear me!

From the sky above
In which thou mayest be,
From the sea beneath
In which thou mayest be.

Creator of the world,
Maker of all men;
Lord of all Lords
My eyes fail me
for longing
to see thee
For the sole desire
to know thee.

O look down upon me
For thou knowest me.

The sun - the moon
The day - the night
Spring - winter,

Are not ordained in vain
By thee, O Deity!

They all travel
To the assigned place;
They all arrive
At their destined ends
Whithersoever thou pleasest.

Thy royal sceptre Thou holdest.

O hear me! O choose me!

Let it not be
That I should tire,
That I should die!

Ancient Peruvian Invocation
From "Pagan Prayers" by Marah Ellis Ryan (1913)

Maia Daguerre

God stir the soil
Run the ploughshare deep
Cut the furrows round and round
Overturn the hard, dry ground
Spare no strength nor toil
Even though I weep.

In the loose, fresh mangled earth
Sow new seed.

Free of withered vine and weed
Bring fair flowers to birth.

Unknown Author

Healing

Our Hands Imbibe Like Roots

Our hands imbibe like roots,
so I place them on what is
beautiful in this world.

And I fold them in prayer,
and they draw from the
heavens light!

Saint Francis of Assisi (1181/1182-1226)
From the book "Love Poems from God: Twelve Sacred Voices from the East
and West" by Daniel Ladinsky

Maia Daguerre

O Supreme and unapproachable Light!

O Blessed Truth,
how far you are from me
who am so close to you.

How distant I am from the sight of you,
though I am present to your gaze.

You are everywhere present
but I see you not.

In you I move and am,
yet I cannot come to you.

You are within me and about me
yet I do not feel your presence.

Anselm of Canterbury (1033–1109)
Benedictine Monk, Philosopher and Founder of Scholasticism

Chapter X

PEACE

Maia Daguerre

Let us know peace.
For as long as the moon shall rise,
For as long as the rivers shall flow,
For as long as the sun shall shine,
For as long as the grass shall grow;
Let us know peace.

Cheyenne Prayer
Native American indigenous people

As wind carries our prayers
for Earth and All Life,
may respect and love light our way.

May our hearts be filled
with compassion
for others and for ourselves.

May peace increase on Earth.

May it begin with me.

Traditional Tibetan Buddhist Prayer

Maia Daguerre

The fruit of silence is prayer.
The fruit of prayer is faith.
The fruit of faith is love.
The fruit of love is service.
The fruit of service is peace.

Mother Teresa (1910–1997)
Roman Catholic Religious Sister and Missionary

Winner of the 1979 Nobel Peace Prize

Lord of Peace, Divine Ruler,
to Whom peace belongs!

Master of Peace, Creator of all things!

May it be Thy will to put an end to war and bloodshed on earth, and to spread a great and wonderful peace over the whole world, so that nation shall not lift up sword against nation, neither shall they learn war anymore.

Help us and save us all, and let us cling tightly to the virtue of peace.

Let there be a truly great peace between every person and their fellow, and between husband and wife, and let there be no discord between people even in their hearts.

Let us never shame any person on earth, great or small.

May it be granted unto us to fulfill Thy Commandment to "Love thy neighbor as thyself" with all our hearts and souls and bodies and possessions.

And let it come to pass in our time as it is written, "And I will give peace in the land, and you shall lie down and none shall make you afraid. I will drive the wild beasts from the land, and neither shall the sword go through your land."

God Who is peace, bless us with peace!

Attributed to Rabbi Nachman ben Feiga of Breslov (1772-1810)

Grandson of the famous Rabbi Baal Shem Tov and member of the Hasidic movement, which combined the esoteric secrets of Judaism ("The Kabbalah") with in-depth Torah scholarship

Maia Daguerre

Deep within the still center of my being,
May I find peace.

Silently within the quiet of the Grove,
May I share peace.

Gently and powerfully,
Within the greater circle of humankind,
May I radiate peace.

Druid Prayer

Very little is known about druids. It is said they were members of the educated, professional class among the Celtic people. Modern historians and archaeologists believe they were religious leaders and shamans (medicine men) of the Celts.

I am peace,
surrounded by peace,
secure in peace.

Peace protects me.

Peace supports me.

Peace is in me.

Peace is mine — All is well.

Peace to all beings,
Peace among all beings,
Peace from all beings.

I am steeped in peace,
absorbed in peace.

In the streets,
at our work,
having peaceful thoughts,
peaceful words,
peaceful acts.

Traditional Buddhist Prayer

Maia Daguerre

Litany for Peace

Praise ye, *Ngai* ... Peace be with us.

Say that the elders may have wisdom and speak with one voice.

Peace be with us.

Say that the country may have tranquility.

Peace be with us.

And the people may continue to increase.

Peace be with us.

Say that the people and the flock and the herds may prosper and be free from illness.

Peace be with us.

Say that the fields may bear much fruit and the land may continue to be fertile.

Peace be with us.

May peace reign over earth, may the gourd cup agree with vessel.

Peace be with us.

May their heads agree and every ill word be driven out into the wilderness, into the virgin forest.

Praise ye, *Ngai* ... Peace be with us.

Traditional Prayer of the Kikuyu People

The Kikuyu are the largest ethnic group in Kenya, Africa.

"Ngai" is the supreme God in their religion, who lives on the holy mountain "Kirinyaga" (Mount Kenya). According to their creation myth, the origin of humanity was fashioned by "Ngai" from a single tree that split into three pieces.

O! Thou God of all beings,

of all worlds, and of all times, we pray that the little differences in our clothes, in our inadequate languages, in our ridiculous customs, in our imperfect laws, in our illogical opinions, in our ranks and conditions, which are so disproportionately important to us and so meaningless to you, that these small variations, that distinguish those atoms that we call men, one from another, may not be signals of hatred and persecution!

Voltaire (1694 –1778)
French Writer, Historian and Philosopher

From the book "Treatise on Tolerance" (1763)

Maia Daguerre

Deep peace I breathe into you,
O weariness, here:
O ache, here!

Deep peace, a soft white dove to you;
Deep peace, a quiet rain to you;
Deep peace, an ebbing wave to you!

Deep peace, red wind of the east from you;
Deep peace, grey wind of the west to you;
Deep peace, dark wind of the north from you!

Deep peace, blue wind of the south to you;
Deep peace, pure red of the flame to you;
Deep peace, pure white of the moon to you!

Deep peace, pure green of the grass to you;
Deep peace, pure brown of the earth to you;
Deep peace, pure grey of the dew to you!

Deep peace, pure blue of the sky to you;
Deep peace of the running wave to you;
Deep peace of the flowing air to you!

Deep peace of the quiet earth to you;
Deep peace of the sleeping stones to you;
Deep peace of the Yellow Shepherd to you!

Deep peace of the Wandering Shepherdess to you;
Deep peace of the Flock of Stars to you;
Deep peace from the Son of Peace to you!

Deep peace from the heart of Mary to you;
And from Briget of the Mantle;
Deep peace, deep peace!

And with the kindness too
Of the Haughty Father Peace
In the name of the Three who are One.

*Fiona Macleod, pseudonym of William Sharp (1855–1905)
Scottish writer*

From the book "From the Hills of Dreams" (1901)

Pray not for Arab or Jew,
for Palestinian or Israeli,
but pray rather for ourselves,
that we might not divide them
in our prayers,
but keep them together
in our hearts.

Unknown Author

Maia Daguerre

Christ, why do you allow wars
and massacres on earth?

By what mysterious judgment do you allow innocent people to be cruelly slaughtered?

I cannot know.

I can only find assurance in the promise that your people will find peace in heaven, where no one makes war.

As gold is purified by fire, so you purify souls by these bodily tribulations, making them ready to be received above the stars in your heavenly home.

Alcuin of York (735-804)
English scholar, Poet and Teacher

The Peace Of "I"

Peace be with you,
All My Peace,
The Peace that is "I",
the Peace that is "I am".

The Peace for always,
now and forever and evermore.

My Peace "I" give to you,
My Peace "I" leave with you,
Not the world's Peace,
But only My Peace,

The Peace of "I".

Morrnah Nalamaku Simeona (1913–1992)
Hawaiian healer

Simeona taught her updated version of Ho'oponopono, an ancient Hawaiian practice of reconciliation and forgiveness, throughout the United States, Asia and Europe.

"I" is the Roman numeral I, representing the oneness of the Universe.

Peace Invocations

Om
May Lord protect us,
May He cause us to enjoy,
May we exert together,
May our studies be thorough and faithful,
May we never quarrel with each other.
Om Shanti
Shanti
Shanti

∼

Om
May there be peace in the sky and in space.
May there be peace on land and in the waters.
May herbs and food bring us peace.
May all the personifications of God bring us peace.
May God bring us peace.
May there be peace throughout the world.
May the peace be peaceful.
May God give me such peace.
Om Shanti
Shanti
Shanti

Traditional Hindu Prayers

Hindu teachings typically end with the words "Om shanti shanti shanti" as an invocation of peace, and the mantra is also used to conclude some Buddhist devotional ceremonies. In Buddhism as well as in Hinduism the threefold "Shanti" is generally interpreted as meaning the Threefold Peace in body, speech, and mind (peace in the entirety of one's being).

Silence

I weave a silence onto my lips.
I weave a silence into my mind.
I weave a silence within my heart.

I close my ears to distractions.
I close my eyes to attractions.
I close my eyes to temptations.

Calm me, O Lord, as you stilled the storm.
Still me, O Lord, keep me from harm.
Let all tumult within me cease.
Enfold me, Lord, in your peace.

Celtic Christian Oral Tradition

Chapter XI

PROTECTION

Hymn to Cihuacoatl

Serpent Woman, plumed with eagle feathers, with the crest of eagles, comes, beating her drum, from the Place of the Old.

She alone, who is our flesh, goddess of the fields and shrubs, is strong to support us.

Our mother is as twelve eagles, goddess of drums calling the gods, filling the fields.

She is our mother - a goddess of war, our mother, a companion from the Home of Ancestors.

She comes forth, she appears when war is waged, she protects us in war that we be not destroyed - an example and companion from the Home of the Ancestors.

She comes adorned in the ancient manner with the eagle's crest, in the ancient manner with the eagle's crest!

Aztec Prayer (14th / 16th century CE)

From the book "Rig Veda Americanus: sacred songs of the ancient Mexicans by Daniel G. Brinton" (1890)

"Cihuacoatl" is the mythical mother of the human race in Aztec mythology. Essentially, a goddess of fertility and reproduction.

Maia Daguerre

Traditional Consecration Prayer to Saint Michael the Archangel

O most noble Prince of the Angelic Hierarchies, valorous warrior of Almighty God, and zealous lover of His glory, terror of the rebellious angels, and love and delight of all the just angels, my beloved Archangel Saint Michael, desiring to be numbered among your devoted servants, I, today, offer and consecrate myself to you, and place myself, my family, and all I possess under your most powerful protection.

I entreat you not to look at how little, I, as your servant have to offer, being only a wretched sinner, but to gaze, rather, with favorable eye at the heartfelt affection with which this offering is made, and remember that, if from this day onward I am under your patronage, you must during all my life assist me, and procure for me the pardon of my many grievous offenses and sins, the grace to love with all my heart my God, my dear Savior Jesus, and my Sweet Mother Mary, and to obtain for me all the help necessary to arrive to my crown of glory.

Defend me always from my spiritual enemies, particularly in the last moments of my life.

Come then, O Glorious Prince, and succor me in my last struggle, and, with your powerful weapon, cast far from me into the infernal abysses that prevaricator and proud angel that one day you prostrated in the celestial battle.

Amen.

Ancient Catholic Prayer
Saint Michael is an archangel in Judaism, Christianism and Islamism. He also plays a special role in many esoteric traditions.

Saint Patrick's Breastplate

I arise today
Through a mighty strength, the invocation of the Trinity,
Through belief in the threeness,
Through confession of the oneness
Of the Creator of Creation.

I arise today
Through the strength of Christ's birth with His baptism,
Through the strength of His crucifixion with His burial,
Through the strength of His resurrection with His ascension,
Through the strength of His descent for the judgement of Doom.

I arise today
Through the strength of the love of the Cherubim,
In the obedience of angels,
In the service of archangels,
In the hope of the resurrection to meet with reward,
In the prayers of patriarchs,
In prediction of prophets,
In preaching of apostles,
In faith of confessors,
In innocence of holy virgins,
In deeds of righteous men.

I arise today
Through the strength of heaven;
Light of sun,
Radiance of moon,
Splendor of fire,
Speed of lightning,
Swiftness of wind,
Depth of sea,
Stability of earth,
Firmness of rock.

I arise today
Through God's strength to pilot me:

Maia Daguerre

God's might to uphold me,
God's wisdom to guide me,
God's eye to look before me,
God's ear to hear me,
God's word to speak to me,
God's hand to guard me,
God's way to lie before me,
God's shield to protect me,
God's host to save me,
From snares of devils,
From temptation of vices,
From every one who shall wish me ill,
Afar and anear,
Alone and in a multitude.

I summon today all these powers between me and those evils,
Against every cruel merciless power that may oppose my body and soul,
Against incantations of false prophets,
Against black laws of pagandom,
Against false laws of heretics,
Against craft of idolatry,
Against spells of women and smiths and wizards,
Against every knowledge that corrupts man's body and soul.

Christ to shield me today,
Against poising, against burning,
Against drowning, against wounding,
So there come to me abundance of reward.

Christ with me,
Christ before me,
Christ behind me,
Christ in me,
Christ beneath me,
Christ above me,
Christ on my right,
Christ on my left,
Christ when I lie down,

Protection

Christ when I sit down,
Christ when I arise,
Christ in the heart of every man who thinks of me,
Christ in the mouth of every one who speaks of me,
Christ in the eye of every one who sees me,
Christ in every ear that hears me.

I arise today
Through a mighty strength, the invocation of the Trinity,
Through belief in the threeness,
Through confession of the oneness
Of the Creator of Creation.

Christian Hymn (5th century BCE)

Although Christian in content, this prayer shows druidic influence, and its original old Irish lyrics were traditionally attributed to Saint Patrick during his Irish ministry.

Translated into English verse by Cecil Frances Alexander in 1889.

Maia Daguerre

Walk in Beauty

Today I will walk out.
Today everything unnecessary will leave me.
I will be as I was before.
I will have a cool breeze over my body.
I will have a light body.
I will be happy forever,
Nothing will hinder me.

I walk with beauty before me.
I walk with beauty behind me.
I walk with beauty below me.
I walk with beauty above me.
I walk with beauty around me.
My words will be beautiful.

In beauty all day long, may I walk.
Through the returning seasons, may I walk.
On the trail marked with pollen, may I walk.
With dew about my feet, may I walk.

With beauty before me, may I walk.
With beauty behind me, may I walk.
With beauty below me, may I walk.
With beauty above me, may I walk.
With beauty all around me, may I walk.

In old age wandering on a trail of beauty,
lively, may I walk.

In old age wandering on a trail of beauty,
living again, may I walk.

My words will be beautiful.

Navajo Prayer
Native American indigenous people

"Walk in beauty" is a crucial concept in Navajo philosophy. For them, beauty means more than outward appearance; it means order, harmony, blessedness and pleasantness. It's their view of how to live a proper life.

Prayer of Light

O Allah!

Grant me Light in my heart,
Light in my grave,
Light in front of me,
Light behind me,
Light to my right,
Light to my left,
Light above me,
Light below me,
Light in my ears,
Light in my eyes,
Light on my skin,
Light in my hair,
Light within my flesh,
Light in my blood,
Light in my bones.

O Allah!
Increase my Light everywhere.

O Allah!
Grant me Light in my heart,
Light on my tongue,
Light in my eyes,
Light in my ears,
Light to my right,
Light to my left,
Light above me,
Light below me,
Light in front of me,
Light behind me,
And Light within myself;

Increase my Light.

Traditional Islamic Prayer attributed to Prophet Muhammad (570-632)

Maia Daguerre

The Great Invocation

From the point of Light within the Mind of God
Let light stream forth into the minds of men.
Let Light descend on Earth.
From the point of Love within the Heart of God
Let love stream forth into the hearts of men.
May Christ return to Earth.
From the center where the Will of God is known
Let purpose guide the little wills of men;
The purpose that the Masters know and serve.
From the center which we call the race of men
Let the Plan of Love and Light work out.
And may it seal the door where evil dwells.
Let Light and Love and Power restore the Plan on Earth.

Ascended Master Djwhal Khul chanelled by Alice Bailey in 1945

Mystic prayer translated into more than 75 languages given to aid the planet during difficult period of planetary changes and readjustments. According to the Theosophists and other scholars of secret texts, it has a mantric formula and its use invokes divine energies of light, love and spiritual power for all humanity.

An Ascended Master is a Being of Light who is not in body. They have paid all their karma, left the cycle of rebirth and attained mastery over themselves.

Psalm 23

Yahweh is my shepherd:
  I shall lack nothing.

He makes me lie down in green pastures.
  He leads me beside still waters.

He restores my soul.
  He guides me in the paths of righteousness for his name's sake.

Even though I walk through the valley of the shadow of death,
  I will fear no evil, for you are with me.
Your rod and your staff,
  they comfort me.

You prepare a table before me
  in the presence of my enemies.
You anoint my head with oil.
  My cup runs over.

Surely goodness and loving kindness shall follow me
  all the days of my life,
    and I will dwell in Yahweh's house forever.

Attributed to King David (10th century BCE)
From "The Book of Psalms"

Maia Daguerre

I, the servant of God, will make fast thrice

nine locks. I take out from the thrice nine locks the thrice nine keys. I fling those keys into the clear ocean-sea; and from that sea will come out a golden-finned, copper-scaled pike, and will swallow my seven-and-twenty keys, and will sink into the depth of the sea. And no one shall catch that pike, or find out the seven-and-twenty keys, or open the locks, or do hurt to me the servant of God.

Ancient Slavonic Spell

Dua Qu'nut

O Allah, make me among those whom You have guided, and make me among those whom You have saved, and make me among those whom You have chosen, and bless whatever you have given me, and protect me from the evil which you have decreed;

Verily, You decide the things and nobody can decide against You; and none whom You have committed to Your care shall be humiliated and none whom You have taken as an enemy shall taste glory.

You are blessed, our Lord, and Exalted, we ask for Your forgiveness and turn to You.

Peace and mercy of Allah be upon the Prophet.

Traditional Islamic Prayer

Maia Daguerre

Psalm 27:1-13

Yahweh is my light and my salvation.
    Whom shall I fear?
Yahweh is the strength of my life.
    Of whom shall I be afraid?

When evildoers came at me to eat up my flesh,
    even my adversaries and my foes, they stumbled and fell.

Though an army should encamp against me,
    my heart shall not fear.
Though war should rise against me,
    even then I will be confident.

One thing I have asked of Yahweh, that I will seek after,
    that I may dwell in Yahweh's house all the days of my life,
    to see Yahweh's beauty,
    and to inquire in his temple.

For in the day of trouble he will keep me secretly in his pavilion.
    In the covert of his tabernacle he will hide me.
    He will lift me up on a rock.

Now my head will be lifted up above my enemies around me.
I will offer sacrifices of joy in his tent.
    I will sing, yes, I will sing praises to Yahweh.

Hear, Yahweh, when I cry with my voice.
    Have mercy also on me, and answer me.

When you said, "Seek my face,"
    my heart said to you, "I will seek your face, Yahweh."

Don't hide your face from me.
    Don't put your servant away in anger.
You have been my help.
    Don't abandon me,
    neither forsake me, God of my salvation.

When my father and my mother forsake me,
    then Yahweh will take me up.

Teach me your way, Yahweh.
    Lead me in a straight path, because of my enemies.

Don't deliver me over to the desire of my adversaries,
    for false witnesses have risen up against me,
    such as breathe out cruelty.

I am still confident of this:
    I will see the goodness of Yahweh in the land of the living.

Attributed to King David (10th century BCE)
From "The Book of Psalms"

Maia Daguerre

Tube of Light

Beloved Mighty "I AM" Presence,
enfold me now in my Mighty Magic Electronic Tube
of Ascended Masters' Light Substance!

Make It so powerful no human creation
can pass through!

See that It keeps me Invisible,
Invincible and Invulnerable
to everything but Thy Almighty Perfection;
Infinitely and Divinely Sensitive to Thee
and Thy Divine Perfection,
Beloved Mighty "I AM" Presence,
and eternally non-recordant
to human creation!

Saint Germain Foundation

The "I AM" Presence is a sphere of light known to Hindus as Brahma, to Buddhists as the Dharmakaya and to Christians as God the Father. It is the spirit of God individualized for each soul. The "I AM" Presence is surrounded by seven concentric spheres of cosmic consciousness called causal body.

The "Tube of Light" prayer serves as a protection, sealing the aura and the chakras from the heavy weight of darkness that is upon the planet.

An Ascended Master is a Being of Light who is not in body. They have paid all their karma, left the cycle of rebirth and attained mastery over themselves.

Magical Incantation

I have invoked thee, O Sun, in the midst of the high heavens.

Thou art in the shadow of the cedar, and thy feet rest on the summits.

The countries have called thee eagerly, they have directed their looks towards thee, O Friend, thy brilliant light illuminates every land, overthrowing all that impedes thee, assemble the countries, for thou, O Sun, knowest their boundaries.

Thou who annihilatest falsehood, who dissipated the evil influence of wonders, omens, sorceries, dreams, evil apparitions, who turnest to a happy issue malicious designs, who annihilatest men and countries that devote themselves to fatal sorceries; I have taken refuge in thy presence.

Do not allow those who make spells, and are hardened, to arise. Frighten their heart.

Settle also, O Sun, light of the great gods, right into my marrow, O Lords of breath, that I may rejoice, even I.

May the gods who created me take my hands! Direct the breath of my mouth!

My hands direct them also, Lord, light of the legions of the heavens.

Sun, O Judge!

Chaldean Prayer
Small Semitic nation from Babylon disappeared in the 6th century BCE
From "Pagan Prayers" by Marah Ellis Ryan (1913)

Maia Daguerre

Each day and each night
that I place myself under his keeping,
I shall not be forgotten.

I shall not be destroyed.

I shall not be imprisoned.

I shall not be harassed by evil powers.

Saint Brigit of Kildare (453-524)
Ireland Saint

I, God, am in your midst.

Whoever knows me can never fall.

Not in the heights, nor in the depths,

nor in the breadths.

For I am love,

which the vast expanses of evil

can never still.

Hildegard of Bingen (1098-1179)
German Benedictine Abbess, Writer, Composer, Philosopher and Visionary

Maia Daguerre

That Wondrous Star

She is truly like a star,
That noble star of Jacob
whose rays illumine the universe,
shine in the highest heaven,
penetrate the darkest depths,
and spread throughout the earth,
warming goodness like springtime,
burning out evil.

She is that bright and wondrous star
forever raised above the great wide sea
of this world, sparkling with merit,
a shining guide.

Voyager, whoever you may be,
when you find yourself in stormy seas
in danger of foundering in the tempests
and far from land, lest you sink and drown,
fix your eyes on this bright star; call out to Mary.

When temptations blow
or the shoals of tribulation threaten,
fix your eyes on this star; call out to Mary.

When the waves of pride or ambition batter your soul,
of slander or jealousy, anger or lust,
fix your eyes on this star; call out to Mary.

In doubt, in danger, in precarious straits,
fix your mind on Mary; call out to Mary,
Never let her leave you, keep her with you always,
even in thy mouth and in thy heart.

Never abandon her presence, never leave her company,
to win approval in her prayers.

Follow her and you will never lose your way.

Appeal to her and you will never lose hope.

Think of her always and you will never stray.

With her holding you, you cannot fall.

With her protection, you cannot fear.

When she leads, you cannot tire.

With her grace you will safely
through to journey's end.

Then you will know for yourself
why she bears the name: "Star of the Sea."

Saint Bernard of Clairvaux (1090-1153)
French Abbot

Chapter XII

SALVATION

Hail Holy Queen

Hail Holy Queen, Mother of Mercy, our life, our sweetness and our hope.

To Thee do we cry, poor banished children of Eve;

To Thee do we send up our sigh, mourning and weeping in this valley of tears.

Turn then, most gracious advocate, Thine eyes of mercy toward us, and after this our exile, show unto us the blessed fruit of Thy womb, Jesus.

O clement, O loving, O sweet Virgin Mary!

Pray for us, O Holy Mother of God, that we may be made worthy of the promises of Christ.

Hermann von Reichenau (1013-1054)
German Scholar, Composer, Mathematician and Astronomer

Central Prayer in Christian Liturgy

Maia Daguerre

Stenatlihan, You are good!

I pray for a long life.

I pray for your good looks.

I pray for good breath.

I pray for good speech.

I pray for feet like yours to carry me through a long life.

I pray for a life like yours.

I walk with people, ahead of me all is well.

I pray for people to smile as long as I live.

I pray to live long.

I pray, I say, for a long life to live with you where the good people are.

I live in poverty.

I wish the people there to speak of goodness and to talk to me.

I wish you to divide your good things with me, as a brother.

Ahead of me is goodness, lead me on.

Apache Prayer
"Stenatlihan" is the supreme sky goddess in Apache mythology

Salvation

One in spirit,
we invoke thee!

Hail, *Amitabha* of the world!

O would that our merciful teacher, *Sakyamuni*,
and our great Father *Amitabha*
would now descend and be present with us.

Would that the perfect compassionate heart
would now draw near
and receive our offerings.

May the omnipotent and omniscient Holy Spirit
Come to us while we recite these divine sentences.

Ancient Chinese Liturgy

In Buddhism, "Amitabha" is often called "The Buddha of Infinite Light."
"Sakyamuni" is the historical Buddha, Sidarta Gautama.

Maia Daguerre

Litany of the Most Precious Blood of Our Lord Jesus Christ

Lord, have mercy.
Lord, have mercy.
Christ, have mercy.
Christ, have mercy.
Lord, have mercy.
Lord, have mercy.
Christ, hear us.
Christ, hear us.

Christ, graciously hear us.
Christ, graciously hear us.
God the Father of Heaven, have mercy on us.
God the Son, Redeemer of the world, have mercy on us.
God, the Holy Spirit, have mercy on us.
Holy Trinity, One God, have mercy on us.

Blood of Christ, only-begotten Son of the eternal Father, save us.
Blood of Christ, Incarnate Word or God, save us.
Blood of Christ, of the New and Eternal Testament, save us.
Blood of Christ, falling upon the earth in Agony, save us.
Blood of Christ, shed profusely in the Scourging, save us.
Blood of Christ, flowing forth in the Crowning with Thorns, save us.
Blood of Christ, poured out on the Cross, save us.
Blood of Christ, price of our salvation, save us.
Blood of Christ, without which there is no forgiveness, save us.
Blood of Christ, Eucharistic drink and refreshment of souls, save us.
Blood of Christ, stream of mercy, save us.
Blood of Christ, victor over demons, save us.
Blood of Christ, courage of Martyrs, save us.
Blood of Christ, strength of Confessors, save us.
Blood of Christ, bringing forth Virgins, save us.
Blood of Christ, help of those in peril, save us.

Blood of Christ, relief of the burdened, save us.
Blood of Christ, solace in sorrow, save us.
Blood of Christ, hope of the penitent, save us.
Blood of Christ, consolation of the dying, save us.
Blood of Christ, peace and tenderness of hearts, save us.
Blood of Christ, pledge of eternal life, save us.
Blood of Christ, freeing souls from purgatory, save us.
Blood of Christ, most worthy of all glory and honor, save us.

Lamb of God, who taketh away the sins of the world,
 spare us, O Lord.
Lamb of God, who taketh away the sins of the world,
 graciously hear us, O Lord.
Lamb of God, who taketh away the sins of the world,
 have mercy on us, O Lord.

V. Thou hast redeemed us, O Lord, in Thy Blood.
R. And made us, for our God, a kingdom.

Let us pray:
Almighty and eternal God, Thou hast appointed Thine only begotten Son, the Redeemer of the world, and willed to be appeased by his blood. Grant, we beg of Thee, that we may worthily adore this price of our salvation and, through its power, be safeguarded from the evils of the present life, so that we may rejoice in its fruits forever in heaven.

Through the same Christ our Lord.
Amen.

Litany promulgated by Pope John XXIII (1960)

Maia Daguerre

Dowa

Save me, my Lord, from the earthly passions and the attachments that blind mankind.

Save me, my Lord, from the temptations of power, fame and wealth, which keep man away from Thy Glorious Vision.

Save me, my Lord, from the souls who are constantly occupied in hurting and harming their fellow-man, and who take pleasure in the pain of another.

Save me, my Lord, from the evil eye of envy and jealousy, which falleth upon Thy bountiful Gifts.

Save me, my Lord, from falling into the hands of the playful children of earth, lest they might use me in their games, they might play with me and then break me in the end, as children destroy their toys.

Save me, my Lord, from all manner of injury that cometh from the bitterness of my adversaries and from the ignorance of my loving friends.

Amen.

Inayat Khan (1882 – 1927)
Indian Musician, Mystic Philosopher and Founder of The Sufi Movement

Anima Christi

Soul of Christ, sanctify me.
Body of Christ, save me.
Blood of Christ, inebriate me.
Water from the side of Christ, wash me.
Passion of Christ, strengthen me.
O good Jesus, hear me.
Within Thy wounds hide me.
Separated from Thee let me never be.
From the malicious enemy defend me.
In the hour of my death call me
And bid me come unto Thee,
That I may praise Thee with Thy saints
Forever and ever.
Amen.

Medieval Catholic Prayer (14th century CE)

Popularly believed to have been composed by St. Ignatius Loyola, this Catholic prayer takes its name from its first two words in Latin, "Anima Christi", which means "the Soul of Christ."

Maia Daguerre

I have no other helper than you, no other father.

I pray to you.

Only you can help me.

My present misery is too great.

Despair grips me, and I am at my wit's end.

O Lord, Creator, Ruler of the World, Father.

I thank you that you have brought me through.

How strong the pain was - but you were stronger.

How deep the fall was - but you were even deeper.

How dark the night was - but you were the noonday sun in it.

You are our father, our mother, our brother and our friend.

Unknown African Prayer

Clash

The threat to our salvation is the clash of peoples:

Jews and Arabs, offspring of a single father, separated in youth by jealousy, in adolescence by fear, in adulthood by power, in old age by habit.

It is time to break these habits of hate and create new habits:

Habits of the heart, that will awake within us the causeless love of redemption and peace.

Rabbi Rami M. Shapiro (1952-)
American Author

Maia Daguerre

Lord Jesus Christ, whose will all things obey:

Pardon what I have done and grant that I, a sinner, may sin no more.

Lord, I believe that though I do not deserve it, you can cleanse me from all my sins.

Lord, I know that man looks upon the face, but you see the heart.

Send your spirit into my inmost being, to take possession of my soul and body.

Without you I cannot be saved; with you to protect me, I long for your salvation.

And now I ask you for your salvation.

And now I ask you for wisdom, deign of your great goodness to help and defend me.

Guide my heart, almighty God, that I may remember your presence day and night.

Attributed to the Desert Fathers (5th / 6th centuries CE)

Early Christian Hermits and Ascetics Monks who lived mainly in the Scetes Desert of Egypt

Save me, God, from the distraction
of trying to impress others,
and from the dangers of having done so.
Help me to enjoy praise for work well done,
and then to pass it on to you.
Teach me to learn from criticism,
and give me the wisdom
not to put myself at the centre of the universe.

Angela Ashwin (1949-)
English Writer, Speaker and Retreat Leader

From "The Book of a Thousand Prayers"

Maia Daguerre

Aren't you going too far, Lord...
with your respect for human freedom?
Your love extends to all creatures.
But you reserve your special love
for the small, the simple, the poor.
Then how can you bear to see
these millions
of your sons and daughters
living in subhuman conditions
owing to the selfishness
and ambition
of unjust and oppressive minorities?
By now you must have realized
that your cataclysms –
floods and droughts,
volcanic eruptions,
typhoons,
earthquakes –
affect the little ones most of all,
whose life is already
subhuman.
Isn't it bad enough
for them to be crusted
by diseases of human weakness?
How are we to explain
what comes from you?
Is it sufficient to say
that you have given us brains
and teach us how to overcome
natural disasters?

Dom Hélder Pessoa Câmara (1909–1999)
Brazilian Catholic Archbishop serving during the military regime of the country and an advocate of Liberation Theology

From the book "Into Your Hands, Lord"

The Seven-Limb Prayer

Respectfully I prostrate with body, speech and mind;

I present clouds of every type of offerings,
actual and imagined;

I declare all the negative actions
I have done since beginningless time,
and rejoice in the merit of all *Aryas*
and ordinary beings.

Please teacher, remain until cyclic existence ends
and turn the wheel of Dharma
for all sentient beings.

I dedicate the virtues of myself and others
to the great Enlightenment.

Traditional Buddhist Prayer

The 7 seven limbs are supports for prayers and meditation, to accumulate merits and purify negativities. They are:
1) Homage to overcome pride
2) Offerings to overcome miserliness
3) Confession to overcome the 3 poisons of the mind: attachment, hatred and ignorance
4) Rejoicing to overcome jealousy
5) Requesting the Teachings to overcome wrong views and negative karma
6) Petitioning the Lama to Remain to overcome negatives actions of abandoning the Dharma.
7) Dedication of merits for the enlightment of all beings

"Aryas" are all sacred beings

Maia Daguerre

Our God, our help in ages past,
Our hope for years to come,
Our shelter from the stormy blast,
And our eternal home!

Beneath the shadow of Thy throne
Still may we dwell secure;
Sufficient is Thine arm alone,
And our defense is sure.

Before the hills in order stood,
Or earth received her frame,
From everlasting Thou art God,
To endless years the same.

A thousand ages in Thy sight
Are like an evening gone;
Short as the watch that ends the night
Before the rising sun.

The busy tribes of flesh and blood,
With all their cares and fears,
Are carried downward by the flood,
And lost in following years.

Thy Word commands our flesh to dust:
"Return, ye sons of men!"
All nations rose from earth at first
And turn to earth again.

Time, like an ever-rolling stream,
Bears all its sons away;
They fly forgotten as a dream
Dies at the opening day.

Like flowery fields the nations stand,
Pleased with the morning light;
The flowers beneath the mower's hand
Lie withering ere 'tis night.

Our God our help in ages past,
Our hope for years to come,
Be Thou our guard while life shall last,
And our eternal home.

Hymn attributed to Isaac Watts (1674-1748)
English Christian Minister recognized as the "Father of English Hymnody"

Maia Daguerre

I know the path: it is strait and narrow.

It is like the edge of a sword.

I rejoice to walk on it.

I weep when I slip.

God's word is:

"He who strives never perishes."

I have implicit faith in that promise.

Though, therefore, from my weakness I fail a thousand times,

I shall not lose faith.

Mahatma Gandhi (1869-1948)
Pacifist Leader

Employing nonviolent civil disobedience, Gandhi led India to independence and inspired movements for civil rights and freedom across the world.

From the book "My Religion"

Chapter XIII

BLESSINGS

Maia Daguerre

Offering the Mandala

Here is the great Earth, filled with the smell of incense, covered with a blanket of flowers.

The Great Mountain, The Four Continents, wearing a jewel of the sun and moon.

In my mind I make them the paradise of a Buddha,

And offer it all to you.

By this deed,

May every living being experience the pure world.

Traditional Tibetan Prayer

In the Buddhist tradition, this prayer is read before a teaching is given, or when starting a practice. The concept is to understand the value of the teachings or the practice, and the practitioner does the biggest offering one could imagine: the whole universe, for the good of all beings.

The Blessing of Light, Rain and Earth

May the blessing of Light be on you, light without and light within.

May the blessed sunlight shine on you, and warm your heart till it glows like a great peat fire, so that the stranger may come and warm himself at it, and also a friend, and may the light shine out of the two eyes of you, like a candle set in the windows of a house bidding the wanderer to come in out of the storm.

And may the blessing of the Rain be upon you, the soft sweet rain.

May it fall upon your spirit, so that all the little flowers may spring up and shed their sweetness on the air. And may the blessing of the Great Rains be on you. May they beat upon your spirit and wash it fair and clean, and leave there many a shining pool where the blue of heaven shines, and sometimes a star.

And may the blessing of the Earth be upon you, the great round earth.

May you ever have a kindly greeting for them you pass as you're going along the roads. May the earth be soft under you when you rest upon it, tire at the end of the day, and may it rest easy over you, when, at the last, you lay out under it. May it rest so lightly over you that your soul may be out from under it quickly, and up, and off, and on its way to God.

Traditional Irish Blessing

Maia Daguerre

Peace Pilgrim's Beatitudes

Blessed are they who give without expecting even thanks in return, for they shall be abundantly rewarded.

Blessed are they who translate every good thing they know into action, for ever higher truths shall be revealed unto them.

Blessed are they who do God's will without asking to see results, for great shall be their recompense.

Blessed are they who love and trust their fellow beings, for they shall reach the good in people and receive a loving response.

Blessed are they who have seen reality, for they know that not the garment of clay but that which activates the garment of clay is real and indestructible.

Blessed are they who see the change we call deaths as a liberation from the limitation of this earth-life, for they shall rejoice with their loved ones who make the glorious transition.

Blessed are they who after dedicating their lives and thereby receiving a blessing, have the courage and faith to surmount the difficulties of the path ahead, for they shall receive a second blessing.

Blessed are they who advance toward the spiritual path without the selfish motive of seeking inner peace, for they shall find it.

Blessed are they who, instead of trying to batter down the gates of the kingdom of heaven, approach them humbly and lovingly and purified, for they shall pass right through.

Peace Pilgrim / Born Mildred Norman (1908–1981)
American Spiritual Teacher and Pacifist who walked more than 25,000 miles for peace

From the book "Peace Pilgrim: Her Life and Work In Her Own Words"

May every creature abound
in well-being and peace.

May every living being, weak or strong, the long and the small, the short and the medium-sized, the mean and the great;

May every living being, seen or unseen, those dwelling far off, those nearby, those already born, those waiting to be born;

May all attain inward peace.

Let no one deceive another, let no one despise another in any situation, let no one, from antipathy or hatred, wish evil to anyone at all.

Just as a mother, with her own life, protects her only son from hurt, so, within yourself, foster a limitless concern for every living creature.

Display a heart of boundless love for all the world, in all its height and depth and broad extent;

Love unrestrained, without hate or enmity.

Then, as you stand or walk, sit or lie, until overcome by drowsiness, devote your mind entirely to this;

It is known as living here life divine.

Traditional Buddhist Prayer

Maia Daguerre

The Sermon on the Mount

Blessed are the poor in spirit,
    for theirs is the Kingdom of Heaven.

Blessed are those who mourn,
    for they shall be comforted.

Blessed are the gentle,
    for they shall inherit the earth.

Blessed are those who hunger and thirst after righteousness,
    for they shall be filled.

Blessed are the merciful,
    for they shall obtain mercy.

Blessed are the pure in heart,
    for they shall see God.

Blessed are the peacemakers,
    for they shall be called children of God.

Blessed are those who have been persecuted
for righteousness' sake,
    for theirs is the Kingdom of Heaven.

From the Gospel of Matthew 5:3-10 (1st century CE)

May penetrating light dispel the darkness
of ignorance.
May all kamma be resolved and the mind-flower of wisdom bloom in *Nirvana*'s eternal spring.
May all those who are afflicted be affliction-free.
May they be serene through all their ills.
Even if bodily afflictions do not subside, may we all be healed in heart and mind.
May all beings live in peace and harmony.
May they have health and wealth and comforts and friends that are true.
May they have skills, talents, and knowledge and sweet success in all that they do.
May they have joy and happiness in abundance.
May all beautiful, great and noble virtues — of generosity, love, kindness, compassion, patience, fortitude, tolerance, forgiveness, honesty, courage, strength, energy, resolution, determination, resilience, perseverance, consideration, humility, gratitude, contentment, composure, serenity, wisdom, understanding and equanimity — be theirs.
May they attain full wisdom and enlightenment.
May they be liberated from all suffering.

Traditional Buddhist Prayer

The term "Nirvana" is most commonly associated with Buddhism, and represents its ultimate state of liberation from the cycle of death and rebirth.

Maia Daguerre

Blessed is the spot,

and the house,
and the place,
and the city,
and the heart,
and the mountain,
and the refuge,
and the cave,
and the valley,
and the land,
and the sea,
and the island,
and the meadow
where mention of God
hath been made,
and His praise glorified.

Bá'u'lláh (1817–1892)
Founder of the Bahá'í Faith

Monotheistic religion that emphasizes the spiritual unity of all humankind

Bless my enemies, O Lord.

Even I bless them and do not curse them.

Enemies have driven me into Thy embrace more than friends have.

Friends have bound me to earth, enemies have loosed me from earth and have demolished all my aspirations in the world.

Enemies have made me a stranger in worldly realms and an extraneous inhabitant of the world.

Just as a hunted animal finds safer shelter than an unhunted animal does, so have I, persecuted by enemies, found the safest sanctuary, having ensconced myself beneath Thy tabernacle, where neither friends nor enemies can slay my soul.

Bless my enemies, O Lord.

Even I bless them and do not curse them.

They, rather than I, have confessed my sins before the world.

They have punished me, whenever I have hesitated to punish myself.

They have tormented me, whenever I have tried to flee torments.

They have scolded me, whenever I have flattered myself.

They have spat upon me, whenever I have filled myself with arrogance.

Bless my enemies, O Lord.

Even I bless them and do not curse them.

Whenever I have made myself wise, they have called me foolish.

Whenever I have made myself mighty, they have mocked me as though I were a dwarf.

Whenever I have wanted to lead people, they have shoved me into the background.

Whenever I have rushed to enrich myself, they have prevented me with an iron hand.

Whenever I thought that I would sleep peacefully, they have wakened me from sleep.

Whenever I have tried to build a home for a long and tranquil life, they have demolished it and driven me out.

Truly, enemies have cut me loose from the world and have stretched out my hands to the hem of Thy garment.

Bless my enemies, O Lord. Even I bless them and do not curse them.

Bless them and multiply them; multiply them and make them even more bitterly against me: so that my fleeing to Thee may have no return; so that all hope in men may be scattered like cobwebs; so that absolute serenity may begin to reign in my soul; so that my heart may become the grave of my two evil twins: arrogance and anger; so that I might amass all my treasure in heaven; ah, so that I may for once be freed from self deception, which has entangled me in the dreadful web of illusory life.

Enemies have taught me to know what hardly anyone knows, that a person has no enemies in the world except himself.

One hates his enemies only when he fails to realize that they are not enemies, but cruel friends.

It is truly difficult for me to say who has done me more good and who has done me more evil in the world: friends or enemies.

Therefore bless, O Lord, both my friends and my enemies.

A slave curses enemies, for he does not understand; but a son blesses them, for he understands; for a son knows that his enemies cannot touch his life; therefore he freely steps among them and prays to God for them.

Bless my enemies, O Lord.

Even I bless them and do not curse them.

Nikolaj Velimirovic (1880-1956)
Serbian Bishop

From the book "Prayers by the Lake" (1922)

A Birthday Prayer

O Child!

May you prosper, may you live for a hundred springs, summers and winters.

May *Ishwar*, all knowing, all pervading, the source of all knowledge and energy that support this entire universe, grant you material, intellectual and spiritual sustenance for one hundred years again and again.

May you live for a hundred years, eat well and enjoy life.

May you live long and ever grow in physical strength, intellect, wisdom and material prosperity attaining fame and glory in all your endeavors.

O *Ishwar*! Please grant this child the best of knowledge, wealth, strength and courage.

Grant him alertness and caution, good fortune, boundless prosperity, health, life free from obstacles and sweetness of voice.

May every day of this child's life be auspicious.

Traditional Hindu Prayer
"Ishwar" is the Supreme Being

Maia Daguerre

The Four Immeasurables

May all beings have happiness
and the cause of happiness.

May they be free of suffering
and the cause of suffering.

May they never be disassociated
from the supreme happiness
which is without suffering.

May they remain in the boundless equanimity,
free from both attachment to close ones
and rejection of others.

Traditional Buddhist Prayer

The Four Immeasurables, fundamental concept of the Buddhist philosophy, are a series of four virtues and the meditation practices made to cultivate them. They are:
1. Immeasurable love
2. Immeasurable compassion
3. Immeasurable joy
4. Immeasurable equanimity

Dedication of Merit

May all sentient beings have equanimity, free from attachment, aggression and prejudice.
May they be happy, and have the causes for happiness.
May they be free from suffering and causes for suffering.
May they never be separated from the happiness that is free from suffering.

By this virtue may I soon
reach a Guru-Buddha-state,
and lead each and every being
to that state of Buddhahood.

May the precious *Bodhicitta*
not yet born, arise and grow
may that born have no decline
but increase forever more.

In all my rebirths may I never be separated from perfect spiritual masters and enjoy the magnificent Dharma. Completing all qualities of the stages and paths, May I quickly achieve the state of *Vajradhara*.

May anyone who merely sees or hears, remembers, touches or talks to me, be instantly freed from all sufferings and abide in happiness forever.

It is only from the kindness of my Guru that I have met the peerless teachings of the Buddha. Thus, I dedicate all merit so that all sentient beings in the future may be guided by kind and holy Gurus.

Until cyclic existence ends, may the beneficial teachings not be blown away by the wind of superstitions. May the entire world be filled with people who have understood and found firm faith in the true teachings.

Day and night, may I pass the time thinking and examining by what means these teachings can spread in the minds of myself and others.

May all sentient beings - who have all been my mother and father - be completely happy, and may the lower realms be forever empty. May all the prayers of the *bodhisattvas*, wherever they live, be immediately fulfilled.

May the glorious gurus live long, and may all beings throughout limitless space have happiness. By purifying our defilements and accumulating positive potential, may I and all others be inspired to attain Buddhahood quickly.

May I never develop, even a moment, wrong views towards the deeds of my glorious Gurus. With respect and devotion, by seeing whatever actions they do as pure, may the guru's inspiration flow into my mind.

In whatever way you appear, O glorious Guru, whatever your retinue, lifespan and pure-land, whatever your name, most noble and holy, may I and all others attain only these.

In order to follow the excellent examples set by the wisdom of the bodhisattva Manjushriand the always sublime Samantabhadra, I dedicate all virtues to their peerless ideals.

All conquerors of the three times have praised this peerless dedication as sublime. Therefore, I also surrender all roots of my activities to the sublime goals of a bodhisattva.

Traditional Buddhist Prayer

Dedication of Merit is one of the most vital and profound part of spiritual practice of the Buddha's teachings.

"Bodhicitta" is the mind that strives toward awakening, empathy and compassion for the benefit of all sentient beings.
"Vajradhara" is the ultimate primordial Buddha.
"Bodhisattvas "are those who, motivated by great compassion, has generated a spontaneous wish to attain enlightment for the benefit of all beings.

Priestly Blessing

May the source bless you and guard you.

May the Source shed light upon you and be gracious unto you.

May the Source lift its face unto you and give you peace.

Traditional Hebrew prayer recited by Kohanim

The Priestly Blessing, also known as raising of the hands, is recited by "Kohanim", priests descendants of Aaron, brother of Moses, that have been divinely chosen to work in the Jewish Temple and assist others in serving God.

During the course of the blessing, the hands of the Kohanim are spread out over the congregation, with the fingers of both hands separated so as to make five spaces between them. The Jewish tradition states the Divine Presence would shine through the fingers of the priests as they blessed the people, and no one was allowed to look at this out of respect for God.

Chapter XIV

BLESSING THE DAY

O Mother Earth,
who has the ocean as clothes
and mountains and forests on her body,
who is the wife of Lord *Vishnu*,
I bow to you.

Please forgive me for touching you with my feet.

Traditional Hindu Prayer

"Vishnu" is the God of Maintenance and Protection

Maia Daguerre

I am awake,

I see the sun.

I am going to give my gratitude to the sun
and to everything and everyone
because I am still alive...

One more day to be myself.

Don Miguel Ruiz (1952-)
Mexican Author of Toltec Spiritualist and Neoshamanistic Texts

From the book "The Four Agreements" (1997)

Morning Consecration to Mother Mary

My queen, my mother, I offer myself entirely to Thee.

And to show my devotion to Thee, I offer Thee this day, my eyes, my ears, my mouth, my heart, my whole being without reserve.

Wherefore, good Mother, as I am Thine own, keep me, guard me as Thy property and possession.

Amen.

Traditional Catholic Prayer

Maia Daguerre

Listen to the exhortation of the dawn!

Look to this day! For it is Life, the very Life of Life.

In its brief course lie all the varieties and realities of your existence;
  The Bliss of Growth,
  The Glory of Action,
  The Splendor of Beauty;

For yesterday is but a dream,
And tomorrow is only a vision;
But today well lived
Makes every yesterday a dream of happiness,
And every tomorrow a vision of hope.

Look well therefore to this day!

Such is the salutation of the dawn.

Kālidāsa (5th century BCE)
Classical Sanskrit Writer regarded as the greatest poet in the Sanskrit language

Blessing the Day

As watchmen wait for the morning,

So do our souls long for you, O Christ.

Come with the dawning of the day,

And make yourself known to us

In the breaking of bread;

For you are our God

Forever and ever.

Amen.

Excerpt from Mozarabic Liturgy

Archaic dialect that was spoken in those parts of Spain under Arab occupation from the early 8th century CE until 13th century CE

Chapter XV

BLESSING THE NIGHT AND THE DREAMS

Oh Lord

kindly forgive my wrong actions

done knowingly or unknowingly,

either through my organs of action (hand, feet, speech)

or through my

organs of perception (eyes, ears)

or by my mind.

Glory unto Thee O Lord,

who is the ocean of kindness.

Traditional Hindu Night Prayer

Maia Daguerre

In Thy name, Lord, I lay me down

And in Thy name, will I rise up.
O God, Thou art the first and before Thee
There is nothing;
Thou art the last and after Thee
There is nothing;
Thou art the outmost and above Thee
There is nothing;
Thou art the inmost and below Thee
There is nothing.
Waken me, O God,
In the hour most pleasing to Thee;
And use me
In the works most pleasing to Thee;
That Thou mayest bring me
Ever nearer to Thyself.

Attributed to Al-Ghazali (1058–1111)
Muslim philosopher and Mystic of Persia

I reverently speak

in the presence of the Great Parent God:

I give Thee grateful thanks

that Thou hast enabled me

to live this day,

the whole day,

in obedience to the excellent spirit

of Thy ways.

Traditional Shinto Prayer (7th century BCE)

Shinto is the indigenous tradition of Japan. Their followers observe ancient practices of ritual purification, nature worship, and abstinence to honor the "kami" (divine spirits). Shinto is unique among religions because there are no founders, no written scriptures, and no required form of worship. Most remarkable, its believers are encouraged to practice Shinto in combination with other religions.

Maia Daguerre

Blessed are you, Lord our God,
King of the universe,
Who causes the bonds of sleep
To fall on my eyes,
And slumber on my eyelids.

May it be acceptable in Your presence,
O Lord my God, and God of my fathers,
To cause me to lie down in peace,
And to raise me up again in peace,
And suffer me not to be troubled
With evil dreams,
Or evil reflections;
But grant me a calm and uninterrupted repose
In Your presence;
And enlighten my eyes again,
Lest I sleep the sleep of death.

Blessed are you, O Lord,
Who gives light to the whole universe
In Your glory.

Traditional Jewish Prayer

Be our light in the darkness, O Lord,

and in your great mercy defend us from all perils and dangers of this night; for the love of your only Son, our Savior Jesus Christ.

Amen.

Be present, O merciful God, and protect us through the hours of this night, so that we who are wearied by the changes and chances of this life may rest in your eternal changelessness; through Jesus Christ our Lord.

Amen.

Look down, O Lord, from your heavenly throne, and illumine this night with your celestial brightness; that by night as by day your people may glorify your holy Name; through Jesus Christ our Lord.

Amen.

Visit this place, O Lord, and drive far from it all snares of the enemy; let your holy angels dwell with us to preserve us in peace; and let your blessing be upon us always; through Jesus Christ our Lord.

Amen.

Traditional Catholic Prayer

Maia Daguerre

Father of Heaven, whose goodness has brought

me in safety to the close of this day, dispose my heart in fervent prayer. Another day is now gone and added to those for which I was already accountable. Teach me, Almighty Father, to consider this solemn truth, as I should do, that I may feel the importance of every day and every hour as it passes, and earnestly strive to make a better use of what your goodness may yet bestow on me than I have done of the time past.

Give me grace to endeavor after a truly Christian spirit to seek to attain that temper of forbearance and patience of which my blessed savior has set me the highest example, and which, while it prepares me for the spiritual happiness of the life to come, will secure the best enjoyment of what the world can give. Incline me, O God, to think humbly of myself, to be severe only in the examination of my own conduct, to consider my fellow creatures with kindness, and to judge of all they say and do with that charity that I would desire from them myself.

I thank you with all my heart for every gracious dispensation, for all the blessings that have attended my life, for every hour of safety, health, and peace; and of domestic comfort and innocent enjoyment. I feel that I have been blessed far beyond anything that I have deserved. And though I cannot but pray for a continuance of all these mercies, I acknowledge my unworthiness of them and implore you to pardon the presumption of my desires.

Keep me, O Heavenly Father, from evil this night. Bring me in safety to the beginning of another day, and grant that I may rise again with every serious and religious feeling that now directs me.

May your mercy be extended over all mankind, bringing the ignorant to the knowledge of your truth, awakening the impenitent, touching the hardened. Look with compassion upon the afflicted of every condition. Assuage the pangs of disease, comfort the broken in spirit.

More particularly do I pray for the safety and welfare of my own family and friends wheresoever dispersed, beseeching you to avert from them all material and lasting evil of body and mind. And may I, by the assistance of your Holy Spirit, to so conduct myself on Earth as to secure an eternity of happiness in your Heavenly kingdom.

Grant this, most merciful Father, for the sake of my blessed savior, in whose name and words I further address you: *(say The Lord's Prayer).*

Jane Austen (1796–1817)
English Writer

Maia Daguerre

O Allah!

I submit my soul to you,
I entrust all my affairs to You,
I turn my face towards you,
I depend upon You for Your Blessings
Both with hope and fear of You.

There is no fleeing,
There is no escape,
There is no refuge, but with you.

I believe in your divine book which You have revealed
And in Your Prophet whom You have sent.

Traditional Islamic Prayer

Watch thou, dear Lord,
with those who wake, or watch, or weep tonight,
and give thine angels charge over those who sleep.
Tend thy sick ones, Lord Christ.
Rest thy weary ones.
Bless thy dying ones.
Soothe thy suffering ones.
Pity thine afflicted ones.
Shield thy joyous ones.
And all, for thy love's sake.

Saint Augustine (354–430)
Early Christian theologian and philosopher

Chapter XVI

HOUSE BLESSINGS

Into whatever house you enter,
first say, 'Peace be to this house.'

If a son of peace is there, your peace will rest on him;
but if not, it will return to you.

From the Gospel of Luke 10:5 (1st century CE)

Maia Daguerre

O heavenly Father, Almighty God,
we humbly beseech Thee to bless and sanctify this house
and all who dwell therein and everything else in it,
and do Thou vouchsafe to fill it with all good things;

Grant to them, O Lord, the abundance of heavenly blessings
and from the richness of the earth
every substance necessary for life,
and finally direct their desires to the fruits of Thy mercy.

At our entrance, therefore, deign to bless and sanctify this house
as Thou didst deign to bless the house of Abraham,
of Isaac, and of Jacob;
and may the angels of Thy light,
dwelling within the walk of this house,
protect it and those who dwell therein.

Through Christ our Lord.
Amen.

Traditional Catholic Prayer

God bless the corners of this house,

And be the lintel blessed.

Bless the hearth, the table too,

And blessing each place of rest.

Bless each door that opens wide,

To stranger kith and kin;

Bless each shining window pain,

That lets the sunshine in.

Bless the roof tree up above,

Bless every solid wall,

The peace of man,

The peace of love,

The peace of God on all.

Irish Blessing

Maia Daguerre

Birkat HaBayit

Let no sadness come through this gate.
Let no trouble come to this dwelling.
Let no fear come through this door.
Let no conflict be in this place.
Let this home be filled
With the blessing of joy and peace.

Traditional Jewish Prayer

Often inscribed on wall plaques and featured at the entrance of some Jewish homes

Great Spirit,

In lighting this candle we summon love, harmony, peace, and prosperity into this home.

May we be blessed with good health, happiness, success, laughter and abundance.

May this home be a sacred dwelling for my beloveds and me.

May those who visit feel peace, light heartedness and love.
We decree that this home is now shielded from harm, illness, negativity or misfortune.

Thank you, thank you, thank you for bringing divine light, love and energy into our hearts, rooms, and endeavors.

With tremendous gratitude, we thank you for your blessings.

In full faith, with harm to none, and the greatest good for all.

So it is!

Unknown Author

Maia Daguerre

O my guardians, from remote antiquity,
Watch over our home.

From top to bottom;
From one corner to the other;
From east to west;
From the upland to the sea;
From the inside to the outside.

Watch over and protect it;
Ward off all that may trouble our life here.

Hawaiian Prayer

Chapter XVII

MEAL BLESSINGS

Maia Daguerre

Bless all of those who have brought this

nourishment to our table
through their labors and their lives.

~

Precious is the Buddha, the unsurpassable teacher,
Precious is the Dharma, the unsurpassable protector,
Precious is the Sangha, the unsurpassable guide,
To the Triple Gem, object of my refuge,
I make this offering with sincere devotion,
I offer this carefully prepared food
Which pleases the mind with a hundred tastes
To the victorious ones and their successors.
May all living beings be sustained
By the abundant food of meditation!

Traditional Buddhist Prayers

Meal Blessings

Blessed are You, Lord our God,
King of the universe,
Who creates varieties of nourishment.

Blessed are You, Lord our God, King of the universe,
Who creates the fruit of the vine.

Blessed are You, Lord our God, King of the universe,
Who creates the fruit of the tree.

Blessed are You, Lord our God, King of the universe,
Who creates the fruit of the ground.

Blessed are You, Lord our God, King of the universe,
Through Whose word everything comes into being.

Blessed is The Lord our God,
Sovereign of the universe,
Who sustains the entire world with goodness,
Kindness and mercy.

God gives food to all creatures,
For God's mercy is everlasting.

Through God's abundant goodness
We have not lacked sustenance,
And may we not lack sustenance forever,
For the sake of God's great name.

God sustains all, does good to all,
And provides food for all the creatures
Whom God has created.

Blessed is The Lord our God,
Who provides food for all.

Traditional Jewish Prayers

Maia Daguerre

Now that I am about to eat,
O Great Spirit,
Give my thanks to the beasts and birds
Whom You have provided for my hunger;
And pray deliver my sorrow
That living things must make a sacrifice
For my comfort and well-being.
Let the feather of corn spring up in its time
And let it not wither
But make full grains for the fires of our cooking pots,
Now that I am about to eat.

Attributed to Native American Tradition

This ritual is one.

The food is one.

We who offer the food are one.

The fire of hunger is also one.

All action is one.

We who understand this are one.

Traditional Hindu Prayer

Maia Daguerre

The food which we are about to eat
Is Earth, Water and Sun,
Compounded through the alchemy
Of many plants.
Therefore Earth, Water and Sun
Will become part of us.
This food is also the fruit
Of the labor of many beings
And creatures.
We are grateful for it.
May it give us strength, health, joy.
And may it increase our love.

Unitarian Universalist Prayer

Liberal and syncretic religion that does not share a creed and whose members are free to seek inspiration and derive insight from all major world religions.

Round the table

Peace and joy prevail.

May all who share
This season's delight
Enjoy countless more.

Chinese Blessing

Maia Daguerre

Innumerable labors brought us this food;
We should know how it comes to us.

Receiving this offering, we should consider
Whether our virtue and practice deserve it.

Desiring the natural order of mind,
We should be free from greed, hate, and delusion.

We eat to support life and to practice the way of Buddha.

This food is for the Three Treasures,
for our teachers, family and all people,
and for all beings in the six worlds.

The first portion is to avoid all evil.

The second is to do all good.

The third is to save all beings.

Thus we eat this food and awaken with everyone.

Mealtime Chant at Zen Buddhist Centers

Chapter XVIII

SAFE JOURNEY

Maia Daguerre

You, O God, are the Lord of the mountains
and the valleys.
As I travel over mountains and through valleys, I am beneath your feet.
You surround me with every kind of creature.
Peacocks, pheasants, and wild boars cross my path.
Open my eyes to see their beauty, that I may perceive them as the work of your hands.
In your power, in your thought, all things are abundant.
Tonight, I will sleep beneath your feet, O Lord of the mountains and valleys, ruler of the trees and vines.
I will rest in your love, with you protecting me as a father protects his children, with you watching over me as a mother watches over her children.
Then tomorrow the sun will rise and I will not know where I am;
But I know that you will guide my footsteps.

Sioux Prayer
Native American Indigenous People

Tefilat HaDerech

May it be Your will, G-d, our G-d and the G-d of our fathers, that You should lead us in peace and direct our steps in peace, and guide us in peace, and support us in peace, and cause us to reach our destination in life, joy, and peace.

(If one intends to return immediately, one adds: and return us in peace)

Save us from every enemy and ambush, from robbers and wild beasts on the trip, and from all kinds of punishments that rage and come to the world.

May You confer blessing upon the work of our hands, and grant me grace, kindness and mercy in Your eyes and in the eyes of all who see us, and bestow upon us abundant kindness and hearken to the voice of our prayer, for You hear the prayers of all.

Blessed are You G-d, who hearkens to prayer.

Traditional Jewish Traveler's Prayer

Maia Daguerre

May the road rise to meet you.
May the wind be always at your back.
May the sun shine warm upon your face.
The rains fall soft upon your fields.
And, until we meet again,
May God hold you in the palm of His hand.

Traditional Irish Blessing

When biding farewell
to someone going off on a journey, recite:

"I make Allah responsible for your deen, your trustworthiness and for the results of your actions."

When some other person undertakes a journey, recite the following:

"May Allah make piety part of your journey, forgive your sins and fulfil the purpose of the journey."

At the time of departure:

"O Allah, let his/her journey be covered quickly and most easily."

By the traveler for the person wishing him farewell:

"I leave your responsibility to Allah in whose protection nothing can be lost when He protects."

Chapter XIX

FACING DEATH

Preserving the Heart

(The chapter of not letting the heart of a man be driven away from him in the underworld)

My heart, my mother; my heart, my mother! My heart of my existence upon earth!

May naught stand up to oppose me in judgment; may there be no opposition to me in the presence of the sovereign princes; may no evil be wrought against me in the presence of the gods; may there be no parting of thee from me in the presence of the great god, the lord of *Amentet*.

Excerpt of an ancient Egyptian prayer

From "The Book of the Dead and other Egyptian Papyri and Tablets" (1901)

Is is written: "This chapter shall be recited over a basalt scarab, set in a gold setting, and placed inside the heart of the man for whom the ceremonies of "Opening the Mouth" and "Anointing with Unguent" have been performed. And there shall be recited by a way of magical charm words: My heart, my mother! My heart, my mother! My heart of transformations!"

"Amentet" is the god of the underworld who receives the dead.

Maia Daguerre

O Creator of men
Thy servant speaks.

Then look on him
The king of Cusco.

Do not forget me
O thou noble creator.

O thou of my dreams.

Dost thou forget
And I on the point of death?

Wilt thou ignore my prayer
Or wilt thou make known
Who thou art?

Thou mayest be what I thought,
Yet perchance thou art a phantom,
A thing that causes fear.

Oh, if I might know!

Oh, if it could be revealed!

Thou who made me out of earth,
And of clay formed me.

Oh look upon me!

Who art thou, O Creator?
Now I am very old.

Inca's Death Prayer

The Inca Civilization flourished in ancient Peru between 1400 and 1533 CE

Do not stand at my grave and forever weep.

I am not there; I do not sleep.

I am a thousand winds that blow.

I am the diamond glints on snow.

I am the sunlight on ripened grain.

I am the gentle autumn's rain.

When you awaken in the morning's hush

I am the swift uplifting rush

of quiet birds in circled flight.

I am the soft stars that shine at night.

Do not stand at my grave and forever cry.

I am not there.

I did not die.

Mary Frye (1905 –2004)
American Housewife

Maia Daguerre

El Malei Rachamim

God full of mercy who dwells on high, grant perfect rest on the wings of Your Divine Presence, in the lofty heights of the holy and pure, who shine as the brightness of the heavens to the soul of _____ who has gone to his eternal rest, as all his family and friends pray for the elevation of his soul.

His resting place shall be in the Garden of Eden.

Therefore, the Master of mercy will care for him, under the protection of His wings for all time, and bind his soul in the bond of everlasting life.

God is his inheritance and he will rest in peace and let us say: Amen.

Central prayer of the Jewish funeral (17th century CE)
"El Malei Rachamim" means "God full of mercy"

Bind the sick man to Heaven,
far from Earth he is being torn away!

Of the brave man who was so strong, his strength has departed.

Of the righteous servant, the force does not return, in his bodily frame he lies dangerously ill.

But *Ishtar*, who in her dwelling is grieved concerning him, descends from her mountain unvisited of men.

To the door of the sick man she comes. The sick man listens! Who is there? Who comes? It is *Ishtar*, daughter of the Moon God! Like pure silver may his garment be shining white! Like brass may he be radiant!

To the Sun, greatest of the gods, may he ascend!

And may the Sun, greatest of the gods, receive his soul into his holy hands!

Ancient Assyrian Pagan Prayer For The Dying

Ishtar is the Goddess of fertility, love, war, sex and power. One of the most famous myths about Ishtar describes her descent to the underworld. It is believed that she can only return from the underworld if she sends someone back in her place.

Maia Daguerre

Blessing

God, omit not this woman from Thy covenant,
And the many evils which she in the body committed,
That she cannot this night enumerate.

The many evils that she in the body committed,
That she cannot this night enumerate.

Be this soul on Thine own arm,
O Christ, Thou King of the City of Heaven,
And since Thine it was, O Christ, to buy the soul,
At the time of the balancing of the beam,
At the time of the bringing in the judgment,
Be it now on Thine own right hand,
Oh! On Thine own right hand.

And be the holy Michael, king of angels,
Coming to meet the soul,
And leading it home
To the heaven of the Son of God.

The Holy Michael, high king of angels,
Coming to meet the soul,
And leading it home
To the heaven of the Son of God.

Ancient Celtic Oral Tradition

Excerpt from the book "Carmina Gadelica" by Alexander Carmichael (1832–1912)

Confession on a Death-Bed

I acknowledge unto thee, O Lord my God and God of my fathers, that both my cure and my death are in thy hands. May it be thy will to send me a perfect healing. Yet if my death be fully determined by thee, I will in love accept it at thy hand. O may my death be an atonement for all the sins, iniquities and transgressions of which I have been guilty against thee, vouchsafe unto me of the bounding happiness that is treasured up for the righteous. Make known to me the path of life: in thy presence is fullness of joy; at thy right hand are pleasures for evermore.

Thou who art the father of the fatherless and judge of the widow, protect my beloved kindred with whose soul my own is knit. Into thy hand I commend my spirit; thou hast redeemed me, O Lord God of truth, Amen, and Amen!

Traditional Jewish Prayer

Maia Daguerre

Prayer of Transformation into a Lotus

Hail, thou lotus! Thou type of the god *Nefer-Temu*!

I am the man that knoweth you, and I know your names among those of the gods, the lords of the underworld, and I am one of you.

Grant ye that I may see the gods who are the divine guides in the underworld, and grant ye unto me a place in the underworld near unto the lords of *Amentet*.

Let me arrive at a habitation in the land of *Tchesert*, and receive me, O all ye gods, in the presence of the lords of eternity!

Grant that my soul may come forth whithersoever it pleaseth, and let it not be driven away from the presence of the great company of the gods!

Ancient Egyptian Prayer

"Nefer-Temu" was, in Egyptian mythology, a lotus flower at the creation of the world, who had arisen from the primal waters.
"Amentet" is the god of the underworld who receives the dead.
"Tchesert' is the holy land, the Other World.

O Saint Joseph whose protection is so great,
so strong,
so prompt before the Throne of God,
I place in you all my interests and desires.

O Saint Joseph do assist me by your powerful intercession
and obtain for me from your Divine Son
all spiritual blessings through Jesus Christ, Our Lord;
so that having engaged here below your Heavenly power
I may offer my Thanksgiving and Homage
to the most Loving of Fathers.

O St. Joseph, I never weary contemplating you
and Jesus asleep in your arms.

I dare not approach while He reposes near your heart.

Press him in my name and kiss His fine Head for me,
and ask Him to return the Kiss when I draw my dying breath.

Saint Joseph, Patron of departing souls,
pray for us.

Amen.

Ancient Catholic Prayer (1st century CE)

Chapter XX

INVOCATIONS OF THE POETS

The Fruit of the Tree

No longer am I
The man I used to be;
For I have plucked the fruit
Of this precious tree of life.

As the river flows down the hills
And becomes one with the sea,
So has this weaver's love flowed
To become one with the Lord of Love.

Go deeper and deeper in meditation
To reach the seabed of consciousness.
Through the blessing of my teacher
I have passed beyond the land of death.

Says Kabir: Listen to me, friends,
And cast away all your doubts.
Make your faith unshakable in the Lord,
And pass beyond the land of death.

Kabir (1398-1518)
Indian Mystic Poet and Saint

From the book "God Makes the Rivers to Flow"
Translated by Eknath Easwaran

Maia Daguerre

It is pure jade, a wide plumage, your heart,
your word, O Father Ohuaya!

You pity man, you watch him with mercy!

Only for the most brief moment is he next to you, at your side!

Ohuaya ohuyaya!

Precious as jade your flowers burst forth, O Life Giver!

As fragrant flowers they are perfected,
as blue parrots, they open their corolas.

Only for the most brief moment next to you, at your side!

Ohuaya ohuyaya!

Nezahualcoyotl (1402-1472)
Mexican Poet

From the book "Ancient American Poets: translations of Nezahualcoyotl and Maya and Inca poets" by John Curl

In the place of tears, I, the singer,
watch my flowers,
they enthrall my spirit as I walk alone with them
- My spirit sad amid the flowers.

In this spot where the herbage is as sweet ointment,
and green as the turquoise and emerald,
I dream of a song of beauty
while the blossoms of beauty are in my hand!

Let us rejoice now, O friends! O children!
For the life of the earth-born is not long upon earth.

I now go forth in swiftness
- to the sweet songs I go forth
- to the flowers of fragrance, O friends! O children!

O *hé*! I sang aloud, O *hé*!
I rained song blossoms as I sped!
Let us go forth to the four ways!

I, the singer, shall find and bring forth the flowers.

Let us be glad while we live - hark to my song of joy!

I, the poet, cry out a song for a place of joy
- a radiant song which descends to the Underworld,
and there turns and echoes back to you!

I seek neither vestments or riches, O friends! O children!
but a song for a place of joy!

Ancient Mexican Poem

Maia Daguerre

Keep off your thoughts from things
that are past and done;
For thinking of the past wakes regret and pain.

Keep off your thoughts from thinking what will happen;
To think of the future fills one with dismay.

Better by day to sit like a sack in your chair;
Better by night to like a stone in your bed.

When food comes, then open your mouth;
When sleep comes, then close your eyes.

Po Chü-I (772-846)
Chinese poet

From the book "More Translations from the Chinese" by Arthur Waley (1919)

Measure for Measure

Isabella: Merciful heaven, Thou rather with thy sharp and sulphurous bolt splits the unwedgeable and gnarled oak than the soft myrtle; but man, proud man, dress'd in a little brief authority, most ignorant of what he's most assur'd —his glassy essence — like an angry ape plays such fantastic tricks before high heaven as makes the angels weep; who, with our spleens, would all themselves laugh mortal.
Act 2, scene 2, 114–123

~

Hamlet

Hamlet: O, that this too too solid flesh would melt thaw and resolve itself into a dew! Or that the everlasting had not fix'd his canon 'gainst self-slaughter! O God! God! How weary, stale, flat and unprofitable, seem to me all the uses of this world! Fie on't! ah fie! 'tis an unweeded garden, that grows to seed; things rank and gross in nature possess it merely. That it should come to this!
Act 1, Scene 2, 129-138

Shakespeare Excerpts (1564-1616)

Maia Daguerre

Part One: Life / LIII

God gave a loaf to every bird,
But just a crumb to me;
I dare not eat it, though I starve, -
My poignant luxury
To own it, touch it, prove the feat
That made the pellet mine, -
Too happy in my sparrow chance
For ampler coveting.

It might be famine all around,
I could not miss an ear,
Such plenty smiles upon my board,
My garner shows so fair.
I wonder how the rich may feel, -
An Indiaman - an Earl?
I deem that I with but a crumb
Am sovereign of them all.

Emily Dickinson (1830–1886)
American Poet

From the book "Complete Poems" (1924)

A Suspended Blue Ocean

The sky
Is a suspended blue ocean.

The stars are the fish
That swim.

The planets are the white whales
I sometimes hitch a ride on,

And the sun and all light
Have forever fused themselves

Into my heart and upon
My skin.

There is only one rule
On this Wild Playground,

For every sign Hafez has ever seen
Reads the same.

They all say,
"Have fun, my dear; my dear, have fun,

In the Beloved's Divine
Game,

O, in the Beloved's
Wonderful
Game."

Hafiz (1325/26–1389/90)
Persian poet

From the book "The Subject Tonight Is Love" by Daniel Ladinsky

Maia Daguerre

Impermanence

Since that far day when Heaven and Earth were new,
Plain to mankind hath been the certainty
That this our world is all impermanence.

Gaze on the heavens, and mark the gleaming moon,
That ever waxes, evermore to wane.

The steep hillsides, tree-clad, flow's-wreathed Spring,
Are fair with blossom; but the Autumn comes,
The cold dew falls, and hoar-frosts' searing touch
Sets the hillside aflame with ruddy leaves—
The red leaf falls, and leaves the branches bare!

So with mankind. Too soon the youthful cheek
Loses its freshness, and the jetty hair
Changes its shining darkness into grey.

The smiling morn turns to the tearful eve,
As the wind blows, unseen of mortal eye.

As the tide flows, nor for an instant stays;
So all things pass, and all are mutable,
And I—I weep, and cannot stay my tears!

Yakamochi (718-785)
Japanese Poet
From "The Man'yōshū," the oldest existing collection of Japanese poetry.
Written on April 20th (750 CE)

A Meditation in Time of War

For one throb of the Artery,
While on that old grey stone I sat
Under the old wind-broken tree,
I knew that One is animate
Mankind inanimate phantasy.

W. B. Yeats (1865-1939)
Irish Poet

From the book "Michael Robartes and the Dancer" (1921)

Maia Daguerre

Prayer

Our lady of Useless Tears,
Thine is my heart's best shrine.
I am sick with the gorging years,
I am drunk with the bitter wine
Of having but cares and fears,
Of knowing but how to pine.

It is useless to pray to thee,
But my heart is full of pain.
Thy glance would be charity,
Even if the look were disdain.
Give me that I may be
A child like thine again.

My sense of me is all tears.
I pity my heart too much.
O a cradle for my fears
And the hem of thy garment to clutch!
O wert thou alive and near us,
And thy hand a hand that could touch!

I do not know how to pray.
My heart is a torn pall.
See how my hair grows gray.
O teach my lips to call
On thy name night and day
As if that name were all.

My fathers' faith doth rise
To my lips this sick hour.
I pray to thee with mine eyes
Rosaries of anguish. O dower
My soul with a least sweet lies
Of thy suffering son's power!

I have forgotten the taste
Of faith, and ache for prayer.
My heart is a garden laid waste.
O thy hand on my hair
Like a mother's hand let rest
And let me die with it there!

Fernando Pessoa (1888—1935)
Portuguese Poet

From the book "Poesia Inglesa" (1913)

Maia Daguerre

God Full of Mercy

God full of mercy.
Were God not full of mercy
there would be mercy in the world, and not just in Him.
I, who plucked flowers on the mountain
and looked in all the valleys,
I, who hauled from the hills dead bodies,
can say that the world is empty of mercy.

I, who was Salt King by the sea,
who stood indecisive at my window,
who counted the steps of angels,
whose heart lifted the weights of pain
in the terrible competitions,
I, who use just a small part
of the words in the dictionary.

I, who must solve riddles despite myself
know that were God not full of mercy
there would be mercy in the world,
and not just in Him.

Yehuda Amichai (1924–2000)
Israeli Poet

From the book "The Poetry of Yehuda Amichai"
Translated by Robert Alter

Invocation of the Poets

Where are the tidings of union? that I may arise-
Forth from the dust I will rise up to welcome thee!
My soul, like a homing bird, yearning for Paradise,
Shall arise and soar, from the snares of the world set free.
When the voice of thy love shall call me to be thy slave,
I shall rise to a greater far than the mastery
Of life and the living, time and the mortal span:
Pour down, oh Lord! from the clouds of thy guiding grace.
The rain of a mercy that quickeneth on my grave,
Before, like dust that the wind bears from place to place,
I arise and flee beyond the knowledge of man.
When to my grave thou turnest thy blessed feet,
Wine and the lute thou shalt bring in thine hand to me,
Thy voice shall ring through the folds of my winding-sheet,
And I will arise and dance to thy minstrelsy.
Though I be old, clasp me one night to thy breast,
And I, when the dawn shall come to awaken me,
With the flush of youth on my check from thy bosom will rise.
Rise up! let mine eyes delight in thy stately grace!
Thou art the goal to which all men's endeavor has pressed,
And thou the idol of Hafiz' worship; thy face
From the world and life shall bid him come forth and arise!

Hafiz (14th century)
Persian poet

From the book "Poems from the Divan of Hafiz" by Getrude Lowthian Bell (1897)

This ode is inscribed upon his tomb in Shiraz, Iran.

Maia Daguerre

What is this atom which contains the whole,
This miracle which needs adjuncts so strange,
This, which imagined God and is the soul,
The steady star persisting amid change?
What waste, that smallness of such power should need
Such clumsy tools so easy to destroy,
Such wasteful servants difficult to feed,
Such indirect dark avenues to joy.
Why, if its business is not mainly earth,
Should it demand such heavy chains to sense?
A heavenly thing demands a swifter birth,
A quicker hand to act intelligence.
An earthly thing were better like the rose
At peace with clay from which its beauty grows.
Ah, we are neither heaven nor earth, but men;
Something that uses and despises both,
That takes its earth's contentment in the pen,
Then sees the world's injustice and is wroth,
And flinging off youth's happy promise, flies
Up to some breach, despising earthly things,
And, in contempt of hell and heaven, dies,
Rather than bear some yoke of priests or kings.
Our joys are not of heaven nor earth, but man's,
A woman's beauty or a child's delight,
The trembling blood when the discoverer scans
The sought-for world, the guessed-at satellite;
The ringing scene, the stone at point to blush
For unborn men to look at and say "Hush."

John Masefield (1878–1967)
English Poet and Writer

Excerpt from "Sonnets" (1916)

Spring

Over cherry blossoms
white clouds
over clouds
the deep sky
over cherry blossoms
over clouds
over the sky
I can climb on forever
once in spring
I with god
had a quiet talk.

Shuntaro Tanikawa (1931-)
Japanese Poet

From "The Selected Poems of Shuntaro Tanikawa" translated from the Japanese by Harold Wright

Maia Daguerre

Buddha in Glory

Centre of all centres, core of cores,
almond that encloses and sweetens itself –
everything, reaching to all the stars
is your fruit's flesh: Hail.

Look, you feel how nothing clings to you;
now your shell surrounds the infinite
and there the strong sap dwells and rises.
And from without a radiance assists him

for high above your suns are turned,
whole and glowing, in their orbits.
Yet in you has already begun
what endures beyond the suns.

Rainer Maria Rilke (1875-1926)
Bohemian-Austrian Poet and Novelist

Translated by Luke Fischer and Lutz Näfelt

The Worm's Waking

This is how a human being can change:
there's a worm addicted to eating grape leaves.
Suddenly, he wakes up, call it grace, whatever,
something wakes him,
and he's no longer a worm.
He's the entire vineyard,
and the orchard too, the fruit, the trunks,
a growing wisdom and joy that doesn't need to devour.

~

Let the beauty we love be what we do.
There are hundreds of ways to kneel and kiss the ground.

~

Lord, the air smells good today,
straight from the mysteries within the inner courts of God.
A grace like new clothes thrown across the garden,
free medicine for everybody.
The trees in their prayer, the birds in praise
the first blue violets kneeling.
Whatever came from Being is caught up in being,
drunkenly forgetting the way back.

Rumi (1207–1273)
Sufi Poet and Mystic

Excerpts from "The Essential Rumi"
Translated by Coleman Barks

Maia Daguerre

Image of God
Born of God's breath
Vessel of divine Love
After his likeness
Dwelling of God
Capacity for the infinite
Eternally known
Chosen of God
Home of the Infinite Majesty
Abiding in the Son
Called from eternity
Life in the Lord
Temple of the Holy Spirit
Branch of Christ
Receptacle of the Most High
Wellspring of Living Water
Heir of the kingdom
The glory of God
Abode of the Trinity.
God sings this litany
Eternally in his Word.

This is who you are.

Unknown Author

I am not I

I am not I.
I am this one
walking beside me whom I do not see,
whom at times I manage to visit,
and whom at other times I forget;
who remains calm and silent while I talk,
and forgives, gently, when I hate,
who walks where I am not,
who will remain standing when I die.

Juan Ramón Jiménez (1881-1958)
Spanish Poet
Winner of the Nobel Prize for literature in 1956

From "Lorca and Jiménez: Selected Poems" translated by Robert Bly

Maia Daguerre

Let me not pray to be sheltered from dangers
but to be fearless in facing them.

Let me not beg for the stilling of my pain
but for the heart to conquer it.

Let me not look for allies in life's battlefield
but to my own strength.

Let me not crave in anxious fear to be saved
but hope for the patience to win my freedom.

Grant that I may not be a coward,
feeling Your mercy in my success alone;

But let me find the grasp of Your hand
in my failure.

Rabindranath Tagore (1861-1941)
Indian writer
Winner of the Nobel Prize in Literature in 1913

From the book "Fruit-Gathering" (1916)

O Thou transcendent,
Nameless, the fibre and the breath,
Light of the light, shedding forth universes, thou centre of them,
Thou mightier centre of the true, the good, the loving,
Thou moral spiritual fountain - affections source - thou reservoir,
(O pensive soul of me - O thirst unsatisfied - waitest not there?
Waitest not haply for us somewhere there the Comrade perfect?)
Thou pulse - thou motive of the stars, suns, systems,
That circling, move in order, safe, harmonious,
Athwart the shapeless vastnesses of space,
How should I think, how breathe a single breath, how speak,
if, out of myself
I could not launch, to those, superior universes?

~

I have said that the soul is not more than the body,
And I have said that the body is not more than the soul,
And nothing, not God, is greater to one than one's self is,
And whoever walks a furlong without sympathy walks to his
own funeral drest in his shroud,
And I or you pocketless of a dime may purchase the pick of the earth,
And to glance with an eye or show a bean in its pod confounds
the learning of all times,
And there is no trade or employment but the young man
following it may become a hero,
And there is no object so soft
but it makes a hub for the wheel'd universe,
And I say to any man or woman,
Let your soul stand cool and composed before a million universes.

I hear and behold God in every object,
yet understand God not in the least,
Nor do I understand who there can be more wonderful than myself.

Why should I wish to see God better than this day?
I see something of God each hour of the twenty-four,

Maia Daguerre

>   and each moment then,
> In the faces of men and women I see God,
>   and in my own face in the glass,
> I find letters from God dropt in the street,
>   and every one is sign'd by God's name,
>   And I leave them where they are,
>   for I know that wheresoe'er I go,
> Others will punctually come for ever and ever.

Walt Whitman (1819-1892)
American Poet

Excerpt from "Passage to India"
Excerpt from "Song of Myself"

All taken from the book "Leaves of Grass" (1900)

The Divine Image

To Mercy, Pity, Peace, and Love,
All pray in their distress;
And to these virtues of delight
Return their thankfulness.

For Mercy, Pity, Peace, and Love,
Is God, our father dear:,
And Mercy, Pity, Peace, and Love,
Is Man, His child and care.

For Mercy has a human heart
Pity a human face,
And Love, the human form divine,
And Peace, the human dress.

Then every man, of every clime,
That prays in his distress,
Prays to the human form divine
Love, Mercy, Pity, Peace.

And all must love the human form,
In heathen, Turk or Jew;
Where Mercy, Love, and Pity dwell
There God is dwelling too.

William Blake (1757–1827)
English Poet and Painter

From the book "Songs of Innocence and of Experience" (1789)

Maia Daguerre

No coward soul is mine,
No trembler in the world's storm-troubled sphere:
I see Heaven's glories shine,
And faith shines equal arming me from fear.

O God within my breast
Almighty ever-present Deity!
Life – that in me hast rest,
As I – Undying Life – have power in thee!

Vain are the thousand creeds
That move men's hearts: unutterably vain;
Worthless as withered weeds,
Or idlest froth amid the boundless main,
To waken doubt in one
Holding so fast by thy infinity;
So surely anchored on
The steadfast rock of Immortality.

With wide-embracing love
Thy spirit animates eternal years,
Pervades and broods above;
Changes, sustains, dissolves, creates and rears.

Though earth and moon were gone,
And suns and universes ceased to be,
And Thou wert left alone,
Every existence would exist in thee.

There is not room for death,
Nor atom that his might could render void;
Since thou art Being and Breath,
And what thou art may never be destroyed.

Emily Brontë (1818 –1848)
English Novelist

The book "Poems of Currer, Ellis and Acton Bell", where this poem is found, was published in 1846 by Emily Brontë and her 2 sisters, Charlotte and Anne, in the hope of raising some much-needed cash, and it sold just two copies.

The moon shines in my body,
but my blind eyes cannot see it:
The moon is within me, and so is the sun.
The unstruck drum of Eternity is sounded within me;
but my deaf ears cannot hear it.

So long as man clamors for the *I* and the *Mine*,
his works are as naught:
When all love of the *I* and the *Mine* is dead,
then the work of the Lord is done.
For work has no other aim than the getting of knowledge:
When that comes, then work is put away.

The flower blooms for the fruit:
when the fruit comes, the flower withers.

The musk is in the deer, but it seeks it not within itself:
it wanders in quest of grass.

Kabir (15th century)
Indian Mystic Poet and Saint

From "The Songs of Kabir" translated by Rabindranath Tagore (1915)

Maia Daguerre

Under One Small Star

My apologies to chance for calling it necessity.
My apologies to necessity if I'm mistaken, after all.
Please, don't be angry, happiness, that I take you as my due.
May my dead be patient with the way my memories fade.
My apologies to time for all the world I overlook each second.
My apologies to past loves for thinking that the latest is the first.
Forgive me, open wounds, for pricking my finger.
I apologize for my record of minutes
to those who cry from the depths.
I apologize to those who wait in railway stations
for being asleep today at five a.m.
Pardon me, hounded hope, for laughing from time to time.
Pardon me, deserts, that I don't rush to you
bearing a spoonful of water.
And you, falcon, unchanging year after year,
always in the same cage,
your gaze always fixed on the same point in space,
forgive me, even if it turns out you were stuffed.
My apologies to the felled tree for the table's four legs.
My apologies to great questions for small answers.
Truth, please don't pay me much attention.
Dignity, please be magnanimous.
Bear with me, O mystery of existence,
as I pluck the occasional thread from your train.
Soul, don't take offense that I've only got you now and then.
My apologies to everything that I can't be everywhere at once.
My apologies to everyone
that I can't be each woman and each man.

Invocation of the Poets

I know I won't be justified as long as I live,
since I myself stand in my own way.
Don't bear me ill will, speech, that I borrow weighty words,
then labor heavily so that they may seem light.

Wislawa Szymborska (1923– 2012)
Polish Poet
Winner of the 1996 Nobel Prize in Literature

From "Poems New and Collected: 1957- 1997"
Translated by Stanislaw Baránczak and Clare Cavanagh

Maia Daguerre

God

In the ancient days, when the first quiver of speech came to my lips, I ascended the holy mountain and spoke unto God, saying, 'Master, I am thy slave. Thy hidden will is my law and I shall obey thee for ever more.'

But God made no answer, and like a mighty tempest passed away.

And after a thousand years I ascended the holy mountain and again spoke unto God, saying, 'Creator, I am thy creation. Out of clay hast thou fashioned me and to thee I owe mine all.'

And God made no answer, but like a thousand swift wings passed away.

And after a thousand years I climbed the holy mountain and spoke unto God again, saying, 'Father, I am thy son. In pity and love thou hast given me birth, and through love and worship I shall inherit thy kingdom.'

And God made no answer, and like the mist that veils the distant hills he passed away.

And after a thousand years I climbed the sacred mountain and again spoke unto God, saying, 'My God, my aim and my fulfillment; I am thy yesterday and thou art my tomorrow. I am thy root in the earth and thou art my flower in the sky, and together we grow before the face of the sun.'

Then God leaned over me, and in my ears whispered words of sweetness, and even as the sea that enfoldeth a brook that runneth down to her, he enfolded me.

And when I descended to the valleys and the plains, God was there also.

Kahlil Gibran (1883 –1931)
Lebanese Artist, Poet and Writer
From "The Madman: His Parables and Poems" (1918)

Notes and Acknowledgments

An exhaustive effort has been made to clear all reprint permissions for this book. This process has been complicated. This is a collection that covers a long period in history and also involves many authors. Some of them or his/her representatives couldn't be found, despite our intensive search. If any required acknowledgments have been omitted, it is unintentional. If notified, I will be pleased to rectify any omission in future editions.

All Bible quotations are from the WEB version (World English Bible).

All Qu'ran quotations are translated by the Progressive Muslims Organization.

Chapter I The Spirit Speaks

"I" Am The "I" by Morrnah Nalamaku Simeona - Copyright © 1980 The Foundation of I, Inc. Freedom of the Cosmos.

"Listen! Do not let your time pass idly" by Anandamayi Ma taken from www.srianandamayima.org – permission sought.

Chapter II Reverence

"Salat" - taken from "The Sayings of Hazrat Inayat Khan" with special thanks to Suluk Press/Omega Publications.

"Five-Pointed Daily Prayer of Worship" excerpted from "A Daily Discipline of Worship" by Torkom Saraydarian. Copyright The Creative Trust; published by TSG Publishing Foundation. All rights reserved. www.tsgfoundation.org.

Chapter III Guidance

"O Thou, Who art the Perfection of Love" - taken from "The Sayings of Hazrat Inayat Khan" with special thanks to Suluk Press/Omega Publications.

"Grandfather, Great Mysterious One" is reproduced from "Black Elk Speaks: The Complete Edition" by John G. Neihardt by permission of the University of Nebraska Press. Copyright 2014 by the Board of Regents of the University of Nebraska.

"Heavenly Father, through your Eternal Word" written by Thabo Makgoba for The United Nations Conference on Sustainable Development in Rio de Janeiro, Brazil, on 2012 is used with permission of the author.

"Lord, teach me to pray" by Eddie Askew, taken from "A silence and a Shouting," p. 7, published by The Leprosy Mission, is used with permission.

Chapter IV Forgiveness

"Lesson 122" - The quotation of Workbook Lesson 122 (W-pI.122.1:1-6.,14:3-5) from A Course in Miracles © is from the Third Edition, published in 2007. It is used with written permission from the copyright holder and publisher, the Foundation for Inner Peace, P.O. Box 598, Mill Valley, CA 94942-0598, www.acim.org and info@acim.org.

"Forgiving Father, forgive us for our sins" by Pastor Suzette Caldwell and The Prayer Institute is used with permission of the author.

"The Litany of Reconciliation" is used by permission of the Coventry Cathedral and the Community of the Cross of Nails.

Chapter V Awakening

"Song of Vibhuti Yoga" by Swami Sivananda is used with permission of the publisher ("The Divine Life Society, Rishikesh, India")

"Contemplation On No-Coming And No-Going" reprinted from Chanting From the Heart (2007) by Thich Nhat Hanh with permission of Parallax Press, Berkeley, California, www.parallax.org

"I see no stranger, I see no enemy" by Dr. Inder Singh is used with permission of the author.

"First I thank the Source of all life" by Harriet Kolfalk is used with permission of Randy Kimbro.

Chapter VI Mother Earth

"Four Directions Prayer" - much effort was made to find the author who is called Vera Dery, including seeking information from the Akta Lakota Museum & Cultural Center. We will be pleased to include a full citation in future editions.

"Though my heart desires shield flowers" - Excerpt from "Cantares Mexicanos: Songs of the Aztecs translated by John Bierhorst, with an Introduction and Commentary". Copyright (c) 1985 by the Board of Trustees of the Leland Stanford Jr. University All rights reserved, Reprinted by permission of the publisher, Stanford University Press, sup.org.

"Grandfather, Great Spirit, once more behold me" is reproduced from "Black Elk Speaks: The Complete Edition by John G. Neihardt" by permission of the University of Nebraska Press. Copyright 2014 by the Board of Regents of the University of Nebraska.

"The Prayer for the Earth" by Fredrich Ulrich is used with permission of the author.

"Water flows over these hands" Reprinted from Present Moment Wonderful Moment: Mindfulness Verses for Daily Living (1990, 2007 rev.ed.) by Thich Nhat Hanh with permission of Parallax Press, Berkeley, California www.parallax.org

"Through the Silence of Nature" taken from "The Sayings of Hazrat Inayat Khan" with special thanks to Suluk Press/Omega Publications.

"Four Elements Medicine Wheel Prayer" by Ralph Metzner, is reprinted, by permission, from Allies for Awakening - Guidelines for productive and safe experiences with entheogens. Green Earth Foundation & Regent Press, 2015. www.greenearthfound.org.

Chapter VII Abundance

"Pir" - taken from "The Sayings of Hazrat Inayat Khan" with special thanks to Suluk Press/Omega Publications.

"The Radical Empowerment PowerShift Process" by Colin Tipping is used with permission of the author.

Chapter VIII

"We give thanks to all those who are moved" by Starhawk is used with permission of the author (www.starhawk.org)

Chapter IX Healing

"Nayaz" by Inayat Khan - taken from "The Sayings of Hazrat Inayat Khan" with special thanks to Suluk Press/Omega Publications.

"Prayer to the World" by Rabbi Kushner is used with permission of the author and was published in the March 23rd 2003 edition of Parade Magazine.

"Heavenly Father" and the following excerpts by Yogananda is used with permission of the "Self-Realization Fellowship" – Los Angeles/ USA

Notes and Acknowledgements

"Violet Flames Decrees" are used with permission of the Saint Germain Foundation / www.SaintGermainFoundation.org

"The Guest House" by Rumi, translated by Coleman Barks is used with permission.

"Our Hands Imbibe Like Roots" by Daniel Ladinsky - From the Penguin publication "Love Poems From God: Twelve Sacred Voices from the East and West." Copyright © 2002 Daniel Ladinsky and used with his permission.

Chapter X Peace

"The Peace Of "I" by Morrnah Nalamaku Simeona - Copyright © 1980 The Foundation of I, Inc. Freedom of the Cosmos.

"The Fruit of the Silence" - The writings of Mother Teresa of Calcutta © by the Mother Teresa Center, exclusive licensee throughout the world of the Missionaries of Charity for the works of Mother Teresa. Used with permission.

Chapter XI Protection

"Tube of Light" is used with permission of the Saint Germain Foundation / www.SaintGermainFoundation.org

Chapter XII Salvation

"Dowa" - taken from "The Sayings of Hazrat Inayat Khan" with special thanks to Suluk Press/Omega Publications.

"Clash" is used with permission of the author.

"Save me, God" by Angela Ashwin, 'The Book of a Thousand Prayers', 2002 Zondervan. Used with permission. www.angelaashwin.com

"Aren't you going too far, Lord" by Dom Helder Camara is taken from "Into Your Hands, Lord" published in 1987 by Darton, Longman & Todd, London. Permission sought.

"I know the path" by Mahatma Gandhi taken from "My Religion", copyright 2011 Navajivan Publishing House. Used with permission.

Chapter XIII Blessings

"Peace Pilgrim's Beatitudes," taken from "Peace Pilgrim: Her Life and Work In Her Own Words" - page 167. Courtesy, Friends of Peace Pilgrim - www.peacepilgrim.org. Copyright ©1982, 1992, 1994, 1998, 2004, 2013 by Friends of Peace Pilgrim. This book is copyrighted only to prevent its being misused. People working for peace, spiritual development, and the growth of human awareness throughout the world have our willing permission to reproduce material from this book.

Chapter XIV Blessing the Day

"I am awake" from the book "The Four Agreements © 1997, Miguel Angel Ruiz, M.D. Reprinted by permission of Amber-Allen Publishing, Inc. San Rafael, CA
www.amberallen.com All rights reserved.

Chapter XX Invocation of the Poets

"The Fruit of the Tree" by Kabir - Translated by Eknath Easwaran, founder of the Blue Mountain Center of Meditation, from "God Makes the Rivers to Flow", copyright 1991, 2003; reprinted by permission of Nilgiri Press, P. O. Box 256, Tomales, Ca 94971, www.easwaran.org.

"Is is pure jade" – taken from "Ancient American Poets: translations of Nezahualcoyotl and Maya and Inca poets" by John Curl is used with permission.

"God Full Of Mercy" by Yehuda Amichai - taken from "The Poetry of Yehuda Amichai" edited by Robert Alter is used with permission.

Notes and Acknowledgements

"Spring" taken from "The Selected Poems of Shuntaro Tanikawa Translated from the Japanese by Harold Wright", North Point Press, San Francisco, 1983 is used with permission.

"Buddha in Glory" by Rainer Maria Rilke translated by Luke Fischer and Lutz Näfelt was first published in Cordite Poetry Review and is used with permission.

http://www.lukefischerauthor.com

"Worm's Waking" / "Let the beauty we love be" / "Lord, the air smells good today" by Rumi, translated by Coleman Barks is used with permission.

"'I Am Not I'" by Juan Ramón Jiménez, from "Lorca and Jiménez: Selected Poems". Translation copyright © 1973 by Robert Bly. Reprinted with permission.

"A Suspended Blue Ocean" from the Penguin publication "The Subject Tonight is Love by Daniel Ladinsky". Copyright © 1996 & 2003 by Daniel Ladinsky and used with his permission.

"Under One Small Star" by Wisława Szymborska taken from "Poems New and Collected: 1957- 1997", translated by Stanislaw Baránczak and Clare Cavanagh. English translation copyright © 1998 by Harcourt, Inc. is used with permission.

About the Author

Maia Daguerre is a writer, singer and songwriter. She is 41 years old, but feels she has been here for a thousand years. She was born in Brazil, but is an inhabitant of the world.

She released four albums in Brazil, Europe and US, two of them with her rock band, Telepathique.

Her first novel was published in Portugal, in 2006, by Editora Fenda.

Until 2013, all her works were done under her birth name: Mylene Pires, or Myle Areal.

For four years, she managed a hostel, in her own house in Rio de Janeiro located inside a native forest and just beneath the famous "Christ the Redeemer Statue," who is blessing her ever since.

In 2014, she rented her house to travel around the world. Her first stop was California, where she and her husband, Walter Daguerre, were supposed to stay for only three months. They have never left... yet.

Currently she is working on many different projects as her soul asks her to do: Finishing a DVD she recorded with ancient Portuguese songs. Finishing her second novel "Hoasca," a collection of short stories related to the use of the sacred drink "Ayahuasca" by Brazilian natives of the Amazon Forest. Recording a TV documentary about holy places around the world.

And... Hoping **The Most Powerful Prayers of All Time** brings with it many blessings to all beings.

Index of Titles and First Lines

A Birthday Prayer, 247
A Meditation In Time Of War, 307
A Suspended Blue Ocean, 305
A Warrior's Creed, 105
Address To Supreme Deity, 49
Always we hope, 5
And I saw the river, 177
And I think over again, 97
Anima Christi, 227
Aren't you going too far, Lord, 232
As watchmen wait for the morning, 257
As wind carries our prayers, 187
Be generous in prosperity, 94
Be our light in the darkness, O Lord, 263
Bind the sick man to Heaven, 293
Birkat HaBayit, 272
Birth is a beginning and death a destination, 99
Bless all of those who have brought this, 276
Bless my enemies, O Lord, 245
Blessed are we, 146
Blessed are you, Lord our God, 262
Blessed are You, Lord our God, 277
Blessed is the spot, 244
Blessing, 294
Bodhisattva Prayer for Humanity, 85
Buddha in Glory, 314
But ask the animals, now, and they shall teach you, 130
But I tell you who hear, 12
Christ, why do you allow wars, 196
Clash, 229
Confession On A Death-Bed, 295
Contemplation On No-Coming And No-Going, 91
Dadirri is deep listening, 117

Dedication of Merit, 249
Deep peace I breathe into you, 194
Deep within the still center of my being, 190
Do not stand at my grave and forever weep, 291
Dowa, 226
Dua Qu'nut, 211
Each day and each night, 216
El Malei Rachamim, 292
Every time I feel the spirit, 141
Exorcism of Spirits of Disease, 171
Father of Heaven, whose goodness has brought, 264
Father, Forgive them, 73
First Epistle to the Corinthians, 165
First I thank the Source of all life, 95
Five-Pointed Daily Prayer of Worship, 37
For everything there is a season, 17
Forgive me, most gracious Lord and Father, 76
Forgive me, O Lord, 71
Forgiveness offers everything I want, 72
Forgiving Father, forgive us for our sins, 78
Four Directions Prayer, 109
Four Elements Medicine Wheel, 126
Full of equanimity, 23
God bless the corners of this house, 271
God Full Of Mercy, 310
God in All Things, 24
God of our life, 60
God stir the soil, 182
God, 326
God, there is no God but He, 47
God's Aid, 53
Golden Chain, 96
Grandfather, Great Mysterious One, 58
Grandfather, Great Spirit, 118
Great and Eternal Mystery of Life, 159
Great Spirit, in lighting this candle, 273
Hail Holy Queen, 221
Hamlet, 303 Part One: Life / LIII, 304

HaShem, 128
He is the One who sent down water from the sky, 137
Heavenly Father, 62
Heavenly Father, charge my body, 170
Ho'oponopono Mantra, 83
Hoshbam (Prayer at Dawn), 133
Hymn To Amun-Ra, 42
Hymn To Cihuacoatl, 201
Hymn To The All-Mother, 108
Hymn To The Unknown God, 180
Hymn XXX. To Earth the Mother of All, 129
I am awake, 254
I am not I, 317
I am of the nature to grow old, 69
I am peace, 191
I Am The "I", 21
I bow to the One who has no color, 43
I cannot dance, O Lord, 67
I cleanse myself of all selfishness, 178
I have no other helper than you, no other father, 228
I know the path: it is strait and narrow, 236
I pray to Thee, Almighty God, 40
I reverently speak, 261
I see no stranger, I see no enemy, 93
I tell you, keep asking, and it will be given you, 10
I, God, am in your midst, 217
I, the servant of God, will make fast thrice, 210
If the only prayer you said, 160
Image of God, 316
Impermanence, 306
In a Thousand Forms, 36
In the place of tears, I, the singer, 301
In Thy name, Lord, I lay me down, 260
Innumerable labors brought us this food, 282
Into whatever house you enter, 269
Invocation to Ormazd, 151
Invocation to The U'wannami, 120
Invocation, 169

It is pure jade, a wide plumage, your heart, 300
It's Harvest Time, 140
Keep off your thoughts from things, 302
Khatum, 54
Late have I loved you, 48
Lead me from the unreal, 68
Lesson 122, 72
Let me not pray to be sheltered from dangers, 318
Let us be grateful to people who make us happy, 161
Let us know peace, 186
Listen to the exhortation of the dawn!, 256
Listen! Do not let your time pass idly, 30
Litany For Peace, 192
Litany of the Most Precious Blood of Our Lord Jesus Christ, 224
Looking behind, I am filled with gratitude, 87
Lord Jesus Christ, whose will all things obey, 230
Lord Jesus Christ, you are the sun, 144
Lord of Peace, Divine Ruler, 189
Lord we Praise You for cities and towns, 153
Lord, make me an instrument of Thy peace, 52
Lord, teach me to pray, 66
Magical Incantation, 215
Make Us Worthy, 63
May all I say, 115
May every creature abound, 241
May I be at peace, 86
May penetrating light dispel the darkness, 243
May the road rise to meet you, 286
Measure For Measure, 303
Mind precedes all mental states, 6
Morning Consecration to Mother Mary, 255
Native American Ten Commandments, 8
Nayaz, 167
Nirvanashatkam, 88
No coward soul is mine, 322
Now that I am about to eat, 278
O Allah! I am your servant, 168
O Allah! I submit my soul to you, 266

Index of Titles and First Lines

O cosmic power!, 98
O Creator of men, 290
O God, forgive the poverty, 81
O God, when I have food, 134
O Great Spirit, whose voice I hear, 55
O heavenly Father, Almighty God, 270
O Jesus, my feet are dirty, 103
O Krishna, it is right, 39
O Lord Jesus Christ, 45
O lord my God, 102
O Lord, O God, Creator of our land, 116
O Lord, remember not only the men, 79
O Lord! Make myself such, 61
O Mother Earth, 253
O My Father, Great Elder, 163
O my guardians, from remote antiquity, 274
O our Father, the Sky, 113
O our Mother the Earth, 125
O Saint Joseph whose protection is so great, 297
O Supreme and unapproachable Light!, 184
O Thou transcendent, 319
O! Thou God of all beings, 193
Ode 279, 136
Offer only lovely things on my altars, 9
Offering the Mandala, 238
Oh Lord, kindly forgive my wrong actions, 259
Ohen:ton Karihwatehkwen, 154
One in spirit, 223
Oracle of Sumiyoshi (Prayer of Benevolence), 92
Our God, our help in ages past, 234
Our Hands Imbibe Like Roots, 183
Our Lord, do not mind us, 82
Part One: Life / LIII, 304
Peace Invocations, 198
Peace Pilgrim's Beatitudes, 240
Pir, 135
Praise be unto Thee, O Lord, 77
Pray not for Arab or Jew, 195

Prayer for Repentance, 75
Prayer For Sustenance, 132
Prayer of Light, 207
Prayer of The Sower, 139
Prayer Of Transformation Into A Lotus, 296
Prayer on building a wall, 101
Prayer to Lord Ganesh, 145
Prayer to Our Lady of Guadalupe, 65
Prayer when opening a door, 100
Prayer, 308
Preserving The Heart, 289
Priestly Blessing, 251
Psalm 23, 209
Psalm 27, 212
Psalm 35, 138
Psalm 8, 44
Remain faithful to the earth, my brothers, 31
Round the table, 281
Saint Patrick's Breastplate, 203
Salat al-Istikharah, 57
Salat, 35
Save me, God, from the distraction, 231
Serenity Prayer, 56
Shema Israel, 19
Silence, 199
Sláva, 111
Song of Vibhuti Yoga, 90
Spring, 313
Stenatlihan, You are good!, 222
Surah Al-Fatiha, 41
Surya Namaskar Mantra, 33
Tao never acts, yet nothing is left undone, 22
Tefilat HaDerech, 285
Thanksgiving Day Prayer, 152
That is perfect, 104
That Wondrous Star, 218
The Blessing of Light, Rain and Earth, 239
The Blessing of Unanswered Prayers, 158

Index of Titles and First Lines

The brightness of the sun, 18
The Canticle of the Creatures, 114
The Divine Image, 321
The food which we are about to eat, 280
The Four Immeasurables, 248
The fruit of silence is prayer, 188
The Fruit of the Tree, 299
The garden is rich with diversity, 123
The Golden Verses Of Pythagoras, 25
The Great Invocation, 208
The great sea moves me, sets me adrift, 179
The Guest House, 176
The Litany of Reconciliation, 80
The Lord's Prayer, 50
The moon shines in my body, 323
The mountains, I become a part of it, 119
The Peace Of "I", 197
The Prayer for the Earth, 121
The Radical Empowerment PowerShift, 142
The Sermon on the Mount, 242
The Seven-Limb Prayer, 233
The sun brings forth the beginning, 150
The Ten Commandments, 7
The Tract Of The Quiet Way, 13
The Vision of Enoch, 2
The Wesley Covenant Prayer, 59
The Words that Come Before All Else, 154
The Worm's Waking, 315
This ritual is one, 279
Though my heart desires shield flowers, 112
Through the Silence of Nature, 124
To recite after Salat Alan-Nabi, 74
To The Creative God, 46
Traditional Consecration Prayer to St Michael, 202
Tube of Light, 214
Under One Small Star, 324
Universal Prayer, 64
Valedictory Address, 11

Violet Flame Decrees, 173
Walk In Beauty, 206
Watch thou, dear Lord, 267
Water flows over these hands, 122
We give thanks for all those who are moved, 148
We return thanks to our mother, the earth, 162
What is this atom which contains the whole, 312
When biding farewell, 287
When the wind blows, 172
Where are the tidings of union?, 311
You, O God, are the Lord of the mountains, 284

Index of Authors, Sources and Themes

A Course in Miracles, 72
A Daily Discipline of Worship, 38
A silence and a shouting, 66
Adi Granth, The, 93
Adi Shankara, 89
African Prayers, 116, 163, 192, 228
African-American Spiritual, 141
Akkadian Invocation, 46
Al-Ghazali, 260
Alcuin of York, 196
Alexander Carmichael, 53, 294
Alice Bailey, 208
Allah, 36, 41, 57, 168, 207, 211, 266, 287
Allies for Awakening - Guidelines for productive and safe experiences with entheogens, 127
American Poetry, 304, 319
Anandamayi Ma, 30
Ancient American Poets: translations of Nezahualcoyotl and Maya and Inca poets, 300
Angela Ashwin, 231
Angels, 4, 16, 71, 202, 270, 294
Anselm of Canterbury, 184
Apache Prayer, 222
Arjuna, 39
Arthur Waley, 302
Ascended Masters, 175, 208, 214
Ashanti Prayer, 116
Assyrian Prayers, 49, 293
Australian Prayer, 117
Aztec Mythology, 201
Aztec, 9, 65, 108, 112, 201
Bá'u'lláh, 94, 244
Báb, The, 77

343

Bábism, 77
Babylonian Prayer, 171, 215
Bahá'í Faith, 77, 94, 244
Bhagavad Gita, The, 18, 39, 90
Bible (New Testament), The, 7, 10, 12, 17, 50, 73, 165, 242, 269
Black Elk, 58, 118
Bohemian-Austrian Poetry, 314
Book of a Thousand Prayers, The 231
Book of Exodus, The, 7
Book of the Dead and other Egyptian Papyri and Tablets, The, 289
Buddha, 6, 69, 96, 223, 238, 249, 276, 282
Buddhist Prayers, 6, 23, 69, 85, 91, 96, 121, 122, 187, 191, 223, 233, 238, 241, 243, 248, 249, 276, 282
Cantares Mexicanos, 112
Carmina Gadelica, 53, 294
Catholic / Christian Prayers, 7, 10, 12, 17, 44, 48, 50, 52, 60, 62, 63, 65, 73, 80, 86, 100, 101, 103, 114, 130, 144, 165, 169, 177, 188, 196, 202, 203, 212, 216, 218, 221, 224, 227, 230, 232, 234, 242, 245, 255, 263, 265, 267, 269, 270, 297
Cecil Frances Alexander, 203
Celtic Tradition, 53, 190, 199, 294
Chaldean Prayer, 215
Chanting From the Heart, 91
Cheyenne Prayer, 186
Chinese Poetry, 136, 302
Chinese Spiritual Traditions, 5, 13, 22, 100, 101, 136, 223, 281
Chinook Prayer, 115, 123
Clare Cavanagh, 325
Coleman Barks, 176, 315
Colin Tipping, 143
Complete Poems – Emily Dickinson, 304
Coventry Cathedral Prayer, 80
Dalai Lama, The, 85
Daniel G. Brinton, 201
Daniel Ladinsky, 183, 305
Dead Sea Scrolls, 4
Desert Fathers, The, 230
Dhammapada, The, 6

Dharma, 11, 64, 233, 249, 276
Djwhal Khul, 208
Dom Hélder Pessoa Câmara, 232
Don Miguel Ruiz, 254
Druid Prayer, 190, 205
Earth Path:
  Grounding Your Spirit in the Rhythms of Nature, The, 149
Ecclesiastes, The Book of, 17
Eddie Askew, 66
Egyptian Prayers, 42, 289, 296
Eknath Easwaran, 299
El Malei Rachamim, 292
Emily Brontë, 322
Emily Dickinson, 304
English Poetry, 312, 321, 322
Enoch, 2
Erasmus of Rotterdam, 144
Essene Gospel, The, 4
Essential Rumi, The, 315
Fernando Pessoa, 309
Finnish Mythology, 139
Finnish Prayer, 139
Fiona Macleod, 194
Florence M. Firth, 29
Found in the clothing of a dead child at Ravensbruck
  concentration camp, 79
Four Agreements, The, 254
Four Immeasurables, The, 248
Fredrich Ulrich, Sensei, 121
Friedrich Nietzsche, 31
From the Hills of Dreams, 194
Fruit-Gathering, 318,
Ganesh, 145
George W. Cronyn, 120
Getrude Lowthian Bell, 311
God Makes the Rivers to Flow, 299
Goethe, Johann Wolfgang von, 36
Greek Hymns, 129

Guru Arjan, 93
Hafiz, 305, 311
Hamlet, 303
Harold Kushner, Rabbi, 167
Harold Wright, 313
Harriet Kofalk, 95
Haudenosaunee, 157
Hawaiian Spiritual Tradition, 21, 83, 197, 274
Helen Schucman, 72
Hermann von Reichenau, 221
Hildegard of Bingen, 217
Hindu Prayers, 11, 18, 33, 39, 64, 68, 88, 90, 98, 104, 145, 198, 247, 253, 256, 259, 279
Ho'oponopono, 21, 83
Holy Spirit, 10, 59, 62, 78, 223, 224, 265, 316
Homeric Hymns, 129
Hugh G. Evelyn-White, 129
I AM Presence, The, 173-175, 197, 214
Inayat Khan, 35, 54, 124, 135, 166, 226
Inca Civilization, 290
Inca, 290
Inder Mohan Singh, Dr., 93
Index of Authors, Books and Themes
Indian Poetry, 299, 318, 323
Indian Saints, 30, 85, 170, 299, 323
Into Your Hands, Lord, 232
Inuit People, 179
Inuit Song, 97
Irish Poetry, 307
Irish Spiritual Tradition, 239, 271, 286
Iroquois Confederacy, The, 157, 162
Isaac Watts, 235
Islamic Prayers, 41, 47, 57, 74, 82, 137, 168, 207, 211, 266, 287
Israeli Poetry, 140, 310
Jainism, 61
James Legge, 136
Jane Austen, 265
Japanese Poetry, 306, 313

Japanese Spiritual Traditions, 92, 96, 105-106, 261
Jesus / Christ, 34, 35, 45, 65, 72, 80, 103, 144, 173, 196, 202, 204, 208, 221, 224, 225, 227, 230, 257, 263, 267, 270, 294, 297, 316
Jewish Prayers, 7, 19, 44, 99, 128, 130, 132, 140, 153, 167, 189, 229, 251, 262, 272, 277, 285, 292, 295
Job, The Book of, 130
John Bierhorst, 112
John Curl, 300
John Masefield, 312
John Wesley, 59
John White, 35
Juan Ramón Jiménez, 317
Kabbalah, The, 128, 189
Kabir, 299, 323
Kahlil Gibran, 326
Kālidāsa, 256
Kapadia, S. A., 75
Khorda Avesta, The, 133
Kikuyu People, 163, 192
King David, 44, 138, 209, 213
Kohanim, 251
Krishna, 18, 39
Lady of Guadalupe, 65
Lakota Tradition, 55, 58
Lao Tzu, 5, 22
Leaves of Grass, 320
Lebanese Poetry, 326
Liberation Theology, 232
Litany of Reconciliation, The, 80
Lorca and Jiménez: Selected Poems, 317
Love Poems from God: Twelve Sacred Voices from the East and West, 183
Luke Fischer, 314
Luke, The Gospel of, 10, 12, 73, 269
Lutz Näfelt, 314
Madman: His Parables and Poems, The, 326
Mahabharata, The, 18, 39

347

Mahatma Gandhi, 236
Man'yōshū, The, 306
Marah Ellis Ryan, 42, 108, 139, 151, 171, 180, 215
Marcel Proust, 161
Mary Frye, 291
Matthew, The Gospel of, 50, 242
Measure for Measure, 303
Mechtild of Magdeburg, 67
Meister Eckhart, 24, 160
Mesopotamia, 46, 49
Metaphysical Meditations, 170
Methodism, 59
Mexican Hymn, 108
Mexican Poetry, 300, 301
Michael Robartes and the Dancer, 307
Mildred Norman, 240
More Translations from the Chinese, 302
Morrnah Nalamaku Simeona, 21, 197
Moses, 20, 251
Mother Mary, 65, 218, 221, 255
Mother Teresa, 188
Mount Meru, 23
Mount of Tepeyac, 65
Mozarabic Liturgy, 257
Muslim, 41, 57, 260
My Religion, 236
Mystics, 21, 24, 25, 35, 38, 54, 67, 86, 95, 98, 102, 124, 135, 160, 166, 176, 177, 202, 208, 217, 226, 230, 260, 299, 315, 323
Nachman ben Feiga of Breslov, Rabbi, 128, 189
Native American, 8, 55, 58, 113, 115, 118, 119, 120, 123, 125, 154-157, 159, 162, 186, 206, 222, 278, 284
Native Peoples Prayers, 92, 97, 116, 117, 163, 179, 192, 261
Navajo Prayers, 119, 206
Nezahualcoyotl, 300
Nicholas de Cusa, 102
Nikolaj Velimirovic, 246
Nirvana, 243

Index of Authors, Sources and Themes

Nirvanashatkam, 89
Nobel Prize, 188, 317, 318, 325
Origen of Alexandria, 103
Pagan Prayers, 42, 46, 49, 75, 108, 139, 150, 171, 180, 210, 215, 293, 296
Pagan Rituals, Liturgies and Prayers, 151
Pagan Witchcraft, 150, 210
Paramahansa Yogananda, 170
Passage to India, 320
Path on the Rainbow, The, 120
Paul Carus, 16
Peace Pilgrim, 240
Peace Pilgrim: Her Life and Work In Her Own Words, 240
Peruvian Invocation, 180,
Peruvian Poetry, 305, 311, 315
Philosophers, 5, 22, 24, 25, 29, 31, 34, 35, 45, 48, 54, 60, 102, 124, 135, 160, 166, 169, 184, 193, 217, 226, 260, 267
Po Chü-I, 302
Poems from the Divan of Hafiz, 311
Poems New and Collected: 1957- 1997 by Wislawa Szymborska, 325
Poesia Inglesa, 309
Poetry of Yehuda Amichai, The, 310
Polish Poetry, 325
Pope John XXIII, 225
Pope Paul Vl, 63
Portuguese Poetry, 308
Prayers by the Lake, 246
Present Moment Wonderful Moment: Mindfulness Verses for Daily Living, 122
Priestly Blessing, The, 251
Prophet Muhammad, 168, 207, 211, 266
Psalms, The Book of, 44, 138, 209, 212
Pythagoras, 25, 29
Qu'ran, 41, 47, 82, 137, 168
Rabindranath Tagore, 318, 323
Radical Forgiveness: Making Room for the Miracle, 143
Rainer Maria Rilke, 314

Ralph Metzner, 127
Ralston, W. R. S., 71, 111
Rami M. Shapiro, Rabbi, 229
Rastafari Prayer, 39
Reinhold Niebuhr, 56
Rig Veda Americanus: sacred songs of the ancient Mexicans, 201
Robert Alter, 310
Robert Bly, 317
Rumi, 176, 315
Russian Prayers, 71, 111
Sabbath, 7
Saint Augustine, 48, 60, 169, 267
Saint Bernard of Clairvaux, 219
Saint Brigit of Kildare, 216
Saint Francis of Assisi, 52, 114, 183
Saint Germain Foundation, 175, 214
Saint Germain, 175, 214
Saint Ignatius Loyola, 34, 227
Saint John of the Cross, 177
Saint Joseph, 297
Saint Michael the Archangel, 202, 294
Saint Patrick, 203
Saint Paul, 165
Saint Teresa of Avila, 86
Sakyamuni, 223
Salat, 35
Samuel F. Pugh, 134
Samurai Song, 105
Selected Poems of Shuntaro Tanikawa, The, 313
Shakespeare, 303
Shaman, 55, 58, 118, 179, 190
Shamanism, 55, 58, 109-110, 113, 118, 119, 120, 123, 125, 127, 154, 162, 179, 254
Shantideva, 85
Shi Jing: The Book of Songs, 136
Shin Prayer, 96
Shinto Prayer, 92, 261
Shuntaro Tanikawa, 313

Index of Authors, Sources and Themes

Sidarta Gautama, 223
Sikhism, 43, 93
Sikhs, 43
Simeon Singer, 132
Sioux Prayer, 113, 284
Slavonic Spell, 210
Song of Myself, 320
Songs of Innocence and of Experience, 321
Songs of Kabir, The, 323
Songs of the Russian People, 71, 111
Sonnets by John Masefield, 312
Søren Kierkegaard, 45
Spanish Poetry, 317
Spiritual Exercises, The, 34
Standard Prayer Book, The, 132
Stanislaw Baránczak, 325
Starhawk, 149
Sufi Poetry, 315
Sufism, 35, 54, 124, 135, 166, 176, 226
Sukhavativyuha Sutra, The, 23
Sukkos, 140
Surah Al-Fatiha, 41
Surya Namaskar Mantra, 33
Sutras, 6, 23
Suzette Caldwell, Pastor, 78
Swami Sivananda, 90
Tao Te Ching, 22
Taoism, 5, 13, 22
Teachings of Zoroaster, The, 75
Teitaro Suzuki, 16
Tewa Song, 125
Thabo Makgoba, 62
Thanksgiving, 140, 152, 157, 297
The Subject Tonight Is Love, 305
Theosophists, 208
Thich Nhat Hanh, 91, 122
Thus Spoke Zarathustra, 31
Tibetan Prayer, 187, 238

351

Torah, The, 19, 128, 189
Torkom Saraydarian, 38
Treatise on Tolerance, 193
Tube of Light, The, 214
Unitarian Universalist Prayer, 280
Uvavnuk, 179
Ved Vyasa, Sage, 18, 39
Vera Dery, 110
Violet Flame, The, 173-175
Vishnu, 253
Voltaire, 193
W. B. Yeats, 307
Walt Whitman, 320
Walter Rauschenbusch, 152
Wiccan Blessing, 150
William Blake, 321
William E Orchard, 81
William Sharp, 194
Wislawa Szymborska, 325
Yahweh, 7, 212
Yakamochi, 306
Yehuda Amichai, 310
Yellow Lark, Chief, 55
Yin Chih Wen, 16
Yoga of the Supreme Person, The, 18
Yoga Tradition, 18, 33, 88, 90, 170
Yom Kippur Prayer, 99
Zoroastrian Prayer, 75, 133, 151
Zoroastrianism, 75, 133, 151
Zuni Prayer for Rain, 120

Also Available From

WordCrafts Press

Speaking and Hearing the Word of God
A Speech-Language Pathologist's Perspective
by Rodney Boyd

Morning Mist
Stories from the Water's Edge
by Barbie Loflin

Pondering(s)
Thoughts on Consecration, Worship, Presence, Discipleship
by Wayne Berry

Youth Ministry is Easy!
and 9 other lies
by Aaron Shaver

Chronicles of a Believer
by Don McCain

Illuminations
by Paula K. Parker and Tracy Sugg

www.wordcrafts.net

www.ingramcontent.com/pod-product-compliance
Lightning Source LLC
Chambersburg PA
CBHW021115300426
44113CB00006B/155